MW00811235

LIONS FOR AJAX

LIONS FOR AJAX

NANCY SNYDER

Illustrated by Linda Dougherty

Shepherd Press
Wapwallopen, Pennsylvania

Lions for Ajax

© 2020 Nancy Snyder

ISBN:
Print 978-1-63342-145-5
Mobi 978-1-63342-147-9
ePub 978-1-63342-146-2

Published by **Shepherd Press**
P.O. Box 24
Wapwallopen, Pennsylvania 18660

All rights reserved. No part of this book may be reproduced or utilized in any form or by any means, electronic or mechanical, or by any information storage and retrieval system—except for brief quotations for the purpose of review, without written permission from the publisher.

Unless otherwise noted, Scripture quotations are from the ESV® (The English Standard Version®), copyright © 2001 by Crossway, a publishing ministry of Good News Publishers. Used by permission. All rights reserved.

eBook information: http://www.shepherdpress.com/ebooks

Cover design and book illustrations by Linda Dougherty
Page design by **documen**. www.documen.co.uk
First Printing, 2020
Printed in the United States of America

Endorsements

Lions for Ajax is a jewel of a book. The characters are vital and vibrant, and the protagonists, Joe and Lisa, deal with real-life problems with authentic Christian grace. This poignant work of fiction offers lived experience and sharp theology on a weighty subject: how to parent, shepherd, disciple, and love a child who hates that God made him a boy. This child does not live in a microcosm, but rather, a feet-on-the-floor, gritty Christian family. In the end, the hurt boy becomes the healed boy by learning to follow the crucified and risen Christ. Christian fiction of this merit can heal us of our deepest fears. This book deserves the highest praise and the widest possible readership.

Rosaria Butterfield Author of *Secret Thoughts of an Unlikely Convert, Openness Unhindered,* and *The Gospel Comes with a House Key*

This work of fiction can encourage parents who struggle to teach children whose hearts seem to be closed to other methods of instruction. I hope many will follow in Nancy's footsteps in using storytelling to bring light to hard issues in creative ways.

Amy Baker Biblical Counselor and Ministry Resource Director at Faith Church, Lafayette, Indiana

Lions for Ajax weaves the different perspectives of the characters into a beautiful story that applies important teachings of the Bible to family life. I felt as if I was invited to be a part of the Trellert family, seeing firsthand how Joe and Lisa interact with their children and neighbors. This book gave me a model for discipling my family. It will also help me in my interactions with the non-Christian world—presenting biblical truth and offering biblical help in a loving way. Thank you, Nancy, for writing this wonderful and encouraging book.

Kevin Hamilton Founder and Director, Deaf Biblical Counseling; Minister of Grace Deaf Presbyterian Church

About the Stories

This is a book of stories by members of three families. Each chapter starts with the name of the person whose story it is.

Dedication

To our sons who were born for the roller coaster,
and who loved the children of the City of York with us.

Acknowledgments

TEARS STREAM AS I acknowledge my gratitude:

○ To those persevering people who prayed for our family as we lived a similar story and so empowered us to survive to tell it. Your names are recorded in God's book. He will not overlook your faith and love, and your mercy will be rewarded in heaven.

○ To early readers—Linda and Ben, Lou and Lynn, Tom, Jack, Trish, Ellen, Susan, Gail, Ellis, Emily, Luke, Amelia, Luis, and Arturo—who slogged through the early true-to-life but unbelievable manuscripts and offered helpful advice that shaped and re-shaped its characters.

○ To the students at Logos Academy who curled up in blankets, drew pictures of the story in their magic journals, and enthusiastically asked the following year, "If we're really good, will you read us *Lions for Ajax* again?"

○ To those who prayed this book into the hands of readers— Ann, Joanne, Janice, Traci, Linda, Jack, Cath, Julie, Cindy, Ellen, Rose Marie, Lou, Lynn, Tom, and Lisa—your prayers produced these pages.

○ To Richard Riggall, who ushered this story through the door at Shepherd Press. To the Shepherd Press team—Jim Holmes, Richard and Bonnie Irvin, Linda Riggall, Aaron Tripp, and Thomas Wiley—for your willingness to take gospel risks and your skill in making those risks less risky.

○ To Linda Dougherty, whose skill and creativity spilled out in illustrations that sing with joy and hope.

○ To Dr. Larry Crabb, who freely offered us his support and this transformative advice:

> *I encourage you to keep hoping. Likely your hope will be the bridge that can carry the weight your son*

feels as he moves from protecting himself from terrible fears by resisting his deep masculine energy to expressing all that is within him in the form of movement into a dangerously uncertain and chaotic world.

Think about the woman as glorying in the unthreatened presentation of her beauty to her world. . . . Pray together as husband and wife about how that picture of MAN and WOMAN can be lived out clearly, not by trying hard to do so, but rather by expressing joyfully the deepest part of who you both are: one who moves toward beauty and one who presents her beauty for larger purposes. [Your son], when he sees the symmetry God designed, may find his male soul drawn to playing his part.

Look for movement in [your son], especially in small relational things . . . Taking little risks, moving toward someone who has been unkind with gentle strength—even the smallest, impure movement—let him know it touches something in you as a woman, and in your husband as a man something joyful and respectful is provoked.

I would urge you to not think of [your son] as having a qualitatively different struggle than any boy learning . . . manhood. Think of it as a continuum and [your son] is at the far end of the struggle, but still on the same continuum of all boys.

○ To those beloved friends who may catch glimpses of themselves in this book, these characters are but smoldering wicks to your shooting stars.

○ To our children, who lived this story—even though its plot is pure fiction. You are our balloons swimming in a joyful sky.

○ To Chuck, for cheerfully reading this story so often you think some of its events actually happened. "Moon back, te más."

○ To Christ, my forerunner, who has planted my anchor behind the veil, so my hope is both steadfast and sure in every storm.

○ And to the little boy in the Easter dress—whose anguish prompted me to share this hope.

Contents

Introduction

I DELIGHT IN THE children who sparkle in my city: children aflame with both trauma and triumph. In this story, I wanted to capture the vulnerability and celebrate the vibrancy of these children. If I had succeeded, fireworks would surely burst from each page.

Lions for Ajax is joyfully set in a world where gender is a gift from a wise and loving God to be lived for His glory. I wrote it for children I love who struggle to accept and live their gender as a gift. Some of the characters in *Lions for Ajax* revel in the gift of their gender. Other characters live sham distortions of their gender but find the joy of repentance. Others wrestle with the gift of their gender but take courageous steps to live the wonder of their masculinity or femininity for the glory of God.

The accompanying study guide helps families dig more deeply into the beauty and symmetry of God's good design for gender. It is one thing to weave a tale with a few fence posts amid the backyard flowers. It is another thing to hang signs on the fence posts saying, "This is the way—the joyful way. Walk ye in it." That is the aim of the study guide. May it help children who anguish over their gender to find God-glorifying hope. May it help families to exalt the goodness of God in creating a gendered humanity.

As for where the lions come in, you'll have to read the book to find out!

The Families

Family 1

Joe Trellert	father
Lisa Trellert	mother
Stephen	13 years old
Ethan	11 years old
Matthew	9 years old
Ajax	6 years old

Family 2

Grandma	
Missy	mother
Molly	6 years old
Kylie	5 years old
McKayla	baby

Family 3

Mr. Damon	father
Nikki	9 years old
Janalia	3-year old twin
Pembrook	3-year old twin

Family 1

Lisa   Joe   Stephen   Ethan   Matthew   Ajax

Family 2

Molly   Kylie

Family 3

Nikki

CHAPTER 1

Lions for Ajax

Kylie

I BUMPED INTO AJAX 'cause he stopped. Right in the middle of the sidewalk. He was so busy lookin' at them lions that he didn't even yell at me. Them lions have curly hair. And long tails. Stephen—he's growed up enough to babysit me—and Ethan—he's almost as growed up as Stephen—he catched up with us.

"Look, Molly," Ajax called. Molly's my big sister, only she's not very big.

"I ain't ascareda no lions!" I jumped up the porch steps and patted them lions on the head.

"No one's afraid of those dumb lions," Matthew said.

"I am," Molly said.

"Stephen, catch me!" I jumped off the porch like a baby bird. Stephen catched me in his arms like a nest. Ajax was still looking at them lions. They looked like they wanted to pounce.

"Stay off other people's porches," Lisa said when she catched up to us. She's Ajax and Matthew and Ethan and Stephen's mom.

A wrinkly man came out on the porch and made mean eyes at us. Mostly at me. I grabbed Lisa's hand—just in case. Then I turned 'round and sticked my tongue out at that man.

"Sassy little thing," the man said, shaking his head. "Hair the color of salsa." I sticked out my tongue again. I hate when people talk about my hair. It's red and crazy curly. But I do like salsa—on my tacos. And I hate when people say I'm little. I'm five now. A whole handful. Joe—that's Ajax and Matthew and

Ethan and Stephen's dad—Joe says I've been a handful since I was born. He's silly like that.

"Lisa, can we go to the park again? Can we? Can we?" I asked. "I like swings, and slides, and baby ducks."

"Can they come next time we have baseball practice?" asked Ethan.

"Probably," Lisa agreed, walking so fast I had to run to keep up. "Looks like rain. We better scramble."

At the corner, we had to wait. Ajax turned 'round to look back at them lions. "I like those lions," he said.

"I hate that man," Matthew said, makin' one of his mean faces.

"I'd like to have lions like that," Ajax said.

Molly was lookin' at Ajax lookin' at the lions.

We crossed the street. "Hey, that was my school!" I told them, pointing at the big red building.

"I bet you were the star of your Head Start class!" Ethan said.

"Yep, and now I go to A B C D Good School," I said.

"You go to A. D. Goode School. It's someone's name," Ethan 'splained.

"Eighty is a dumb name," Matthew said.

"It's initials: A and D." Stephen started talkin' like a teacher. "His name was Alexander."

"Alexander—the boy with the no good day?" I asked. Ethan read me that book last night 'fore I sleeped in a sleepin' bag on Lisa's floor.

"No, Alexander D. Goode died so soldiers could get off a sinking ship," Stephen 'splained.

"Like a knight!" Ajax said.

"Like an idiot," Matthew said. Matthew's like that.

Stephen kept 'splainin' on and on. Sometimes Stephen's 'splainin' makes me dizzy, like I just got off the merry-go-round at the fair. Something about a Boy Scout group for boys of different races.

"I like races," Ajax shouted.

"Not those kind of races," Stephen started.

I shouted over Stephen, "Some boys pulled my hair in school." I grabbed Ethan's hand, to make sure he was listening.

"They did? Did your teacher tell them to be kind?" Ethan

asked.

"No, but when I kicked them, my teacher writed my name on the bad list on the board."

"Uh-oh," Ethan said, shaking his finger but still smilin' at me.

"I never get my name on the board," Molly said.

"I always get my name on the board. Maybe your teacher don't know how to spell your name," I said.

"Doesn't," Stephen said. "Maybe your teacher doesn't know how to spell your name."

He must not have been listening, so this time I shouted. "My teacher do know how to spell my name. She does it most every day."

"My teacher knows how to spell everything," Molly said.

"So do I," Ethan said. "E-v-e-r-y . . . "

"My teacher can't spell everything," Stephen said, loud enough for Lisa to hear. Lisa teaches her kids at home.

"And big boys pick on us after school. Big and mean. And they chase me and Molly." I swinged Ethan's hand up and down like the swings at the park. "And they ask mean questions."

"What are mean questions?" Stephen asked.

"Mean questions ain't like, 'What's your favoritest thing to do?' Then I can say, 'Play and smell flowers,'" I said. I bent down and picked a red flower from someone's yard.

"So, what mean questions do they ask?" Stephen said.

"Like, 'Are you a cry baby?' and 'Where'd ya get that hair, red?' and 'How's come you got white skin and kinky hair?'"

"I tried to 'splain' him that our dad is Black and our mom . . ." Molly began.

"We ain't got no dad," I said. "If we did, he could whip them bad boys. But they just keeped on, "Bet you were an ugly baby with ruggedy red hair?"

"I'll teach them a thing or two," Ajax yelled, punchin' his fists at nothin'.

"You should pray for them," Lisa said. She stopped on our front steps and started prayin' right there. Lisa's crazy like that. She prayed for them mean boys. And she asked God to keep us safe. That part was good at least.

"After I teach them a thing or two, then I could pray for 'em," Ajax whispered.

As soon as I opened our front door, Buster jumped up on me. "Wow! Your dog has gotten so big," Ethan said, petting Buster's ears.

"Yep. He used to knock me down. But I holded his face and yelled at him, 'NO!' and blowed up his nose."

"Didn't he bite you?" Ethan asked.

"Nope, and now he don't knock me down no more. But he knocks Molly down all the time. 'Cause she don't blow up his nose and shout, 'No.'"

That night, when Molly and me went to bed, we couldn't sleep. MaKayla—that's our baby sister—she was cryin'. Her crib's right by our bed. So we couldn't sleep. And there was lightnin' outside. It was loud.

Molly said we should pray for those mean boys. I thought she was crazy as Lisa. Then I got a idea. "God, make lightnin' hit them mean boys," I prayed.

Molly didn't think that's what Lisa wanted, but that's what I did. Then Molly started talking 'bout Ajax wantin' them lions. "We gotta get those lions for Ajax," Molly said.

"Okay," I said. "We'll take 'em next time we walk home from school. We'll scare them mean boys. Then we'll give the lions to Ajax. We won't need no lions after we scare them boys."

Molly said taking the lions was stealing. She said, "Next time Mama goes to the store, we'll buy a lion."

I told her that was a dumb idea. "We go at the store with Mama all the time, and we ain't never seen no lions."

"We'll have to ask that man if he'll sell them to us," Molly whispered.

"No way!" I hollered. "He prob'ly eats kids. And we ain't never got no money."

"We could ask Stephen and Ethan to help us," Molly said.

We both knew Stephen and Ethan wouldn't let us steal the lions. "Matthew'd help us steal 'em," I said.

"Matthew doesn't like to help," Molly began.

"But he might like to steal," I said.

Even in the dark, I could see Molly's eyes, big and scared. She was still thinkin' how we could get them lions.

CHAPTER 2

Polite in Three Languages

Stephen

AFTER DINNER MONDAY NIGHT, Dad took a deep breath and pushed back his chair. That meant trouble. "Matthew Trellert." That meant double trouble. Triple trouble is when Dad uses first, middle, and last names—that's our red alert. Dad went on, "Your mom said you were rude to the speaker at the medieval festival today."

We had spent the day with friends from our homeschool co-op having a medieval tournament, sampling medieval foods, and listening to a medieval storyteller.

Matthew squealed, "He was wearing a dress!" He sounded weirdly excited about this.

"It was a tunic," I explained.

"He said that people back then hardly ever took baths," Matthew spat out. "I was supposed to thank him for that?"

Dad lamented, "Matthew, what's it going to take to teach you to be polite to people?"

"I have an idea," Mom said. She's famous for her ideas. "Let's act out some situations and role-play talking nicely to people."

"That's baby stuff!" Matthew yelled.

"If the shoe fits . . ." I began.

"That's a great idea," Dad interrupted, giving me that warning look. "Let's give it a try. Everyone, into the living room. I'll pretend to be different people who come to our home, and each of you kids can say something polite to greet me when I walk in the door." "I'd rather play baseball," Ajax said.

"I'd rather eat dirt," added Matthew, plopping down on the sofa.

"None of that," Dad said enthusiastically. "Now, we'll start with the youngest, and each of you has to think of something different to say. Here goes." Dad walked out the front door and entered back in with a sniffle. "Hi," he said in a high-pitched voice. "I hope I'm not bothering you. Would it be too much to ask if I could borrow your weed whacker?" Dad sniffed again.

We immediately recognized him as Mrs. Graham from down the street. Ethan and I always shovel her sidewalk during winter, but she insists on doing all her own yard work even though she is in her eighties. Dad had taught her to use our weed whacker last summer, telling her to borrow it any time she wanted to trim the grass along her fence.

Mom looked at Ajax, motioning for him to say something polite to Mrs. Graham. "Hi. I'll get the weed whacker." Ajax pretended to grab the weed whacker then bent down on one knee—like a knight bowing before his queen. "At your service," he added while pretending to hand over the imaginary weed whacker.

"Very nice," Mom applauded.

"If a trifle overdone," I added, looking up from the book I was glad I had left in the living room before dinner.

"Matthew, you can think of something to say to Mrs. Graham," Mom said. Dad sniffed, sounding just like Mrs. Graham during hayfever season.

"How 'bout, 'Why don't you use a tissue?'" Matthew said.

Ethan and I started to laugh, but Dad shot us that look. "Matthew, I want you to say something nice to everyone who comes through our door," Dad explained.

"Mrs. Graham doesn't come through the door. She just leans over the fence," Matthew argued.

"Matthew," Dad's voice was getting tight. "You need to say something nice to everyone who speaks to you. Whether they come through the front door, lean over the fence, or drop down the chimney."

"We don't even have a chimney," Matthew complained. "When I get big, I want a fancy house with a chimney, not some dumb row house."

"Matthew, what could you say to Mrs. Graham?" Dad persisted with impressive concentration. Usually that last comment of Matthew's would have sidetracked him, but tonight he couldn't be stopped.

"Hello. How are you?" Matthew said with a twisted face. "That sounds stupid," he whined.

"No, Matthew," Mom said. "It sounds stupid not to answer people who speak to you. Now try it again, in a nice voice."

"Hello. How are you?" Matthew said shrilly.

"In a regular voice, Matthew," Dad barked. This was getting old—ancient, like the Roman Empire, without the excitement of man-eating lions.

"HelloHowareyou?" Matthew said quickly, as if it were one word.

"Good," Mom said, trying to high five Matthew, who was having none of it. "And you, Ethan?"

"I could say, 'Mrs. Graham, let me trim that grass for you,'" Ethan said.

"Yeah, only because you know she wouldn't let you," Matthew sneered.

When Dad turned to me, I was ready. "I could say, 'How is your great-granddaughter? I'll soon be off school for the whole summer, in case you've gotten any new videos of her.'"

Mom and Dad tried to hide their laughter, but I knew they were remembering the time Mrs. Graham had lent us a stack of videos of her great-granddaughter—sitting in her high chair, sitting in her bath, sitting in her car seat, sitting in her swing, and sitting in her infant seat.

"Actually," Mom said, "It would be very thoughtful of you to ask Mrs. Graham about her great-granddaughter."

"And brave," Ajax added.

"You could ask if her great-granddaughter has gotten any new teeth this week," Matthew smirked.

"Guys, remember the idea behind manners is love. Got it? Love," Dad said. "Ready for our next person to greet? Now, I'll pretend I'm out on the street, and you say hi to me." Dad pantomimed scrubbing and waxing a car.

"I know!" Ajax yelled. "You're Damon, washing the car!"

Dad held up one finger, motioning for us to wait a minute. He reached inside the car and pretended to turn down the volume knob on his radio. "Now I can hear you," Dad said.

"Okay, Ajax, your turn," Mom began.

"How 'bout washing mine next, Damon?" Ajax yelled. That's what Dad always says when he sees Damon washing his car, which is often. Mom grinned.

"No, Ajax, I can say that to Damon because he and I are about the same age. That's, 'How 'bout washing mine next, *Mr.* Damon?' for you. Something polite, Ajax."

"Hi, Mr. Damon," Ajax tried again. "Your car really shines!"

"Soon your manners will shine, Ajax," Mom said.

"Like a knight in shining armor," Dad added. "And you, Matthew?"

"I don't talk to Damon. I'm scared of him." Matthew said.

"*Mr.* Damon, Matthew. Please call him *Mr.* Damon. I do lots of things I'm scared to do. Now what can you say to Mr. Damon?" Mom urged.

"Hi, Mr. Damon," Matthew spat out the words. Then he added, "I hate this game."

"We're going to keep playing it until you start talking politely, Matthew." Dad plowed on, "And you, Ethan, what could you say?"

"Hi, Mr. Damon, want me to play with Pembrook and Janalia, so you can finish washing the car?" Ethan said, referring to Damon's—Mr. Damon's—youngest kids, who are twins.

"Great!" Dad answered, still pretending to wash the car. Finally it was my turn.

"I could say, 'If you spent half as much time reading as you spend washing the car, you'd be twice as smart as you think I am,'" I began. Then—seeing that look on Dad's face—I added quickly, "But that would be rude, so instead, I'll say, 'Hi, Mr. Damon, what's up?'"

"Oh, nothing much," Dad-playing-Mr.-Damon replied.

"Due to its ontological status, nothing cannot be, so it is not," I replied. I'd been reading about philosophy lately. But Dad was not interested in philosophy right now and was already moving on.

"Now, here's a practical situation," Dad said. He left the room and walked out the front door. He rang the doorbell twice then pounded on the door. I knew where he was headed with this one. Dad is an interpreter, and Deaf people often come to visit. Ajax ran to open the door. Pretending to be the pastor of the Deaf church, Dad doffed his imaginary hat and signed, "Hi. Is your father home?"

Ajax stood there a second before whispering, "You are my father."

Ethan and I howled. Ajax was about to blow up when Mom helped out. "It's rude to leave people standing out front, Ajax. Let him in and say something nice."

Ajax motioned for Dad to come in, then signed, "Please, sit."

"Good," Mom signed to Ajax, then pointed to Matthew.

"I can't," Matthew said.

"Sure you can," Mom said. "You know lots of ASL." That's American Sign Language, and it's mandatory at our house when Deaf people visit.

"But I feel stupid when I sign," Matthew said.

"But you look stupid if there are Deaf people around and you don't sign," I added, being my usual helpful self.

Finally, Matthew signed, "Dad," then pointed downstairs, to show that Dad was in his basement office.

"Great," Mom said, "Then you could run down and get your dad. Ethan?"

"Your hat?" Ethan asked with a questioning look. Dad, still acting his role, pretended to hand over his hat. "Your coat?" Ethan signed again. Dad took off an imaginary coat. Ethan actually went to the coat closet, pretending to set the hat carefully on the shelf and ceremoniously drape the coat over a hanger. This was starting to look like father and son Academy Awards in the making.

Dad looked at me, and I signed the speech I had been planning. "Welcome. In honor of your pastoral presence, we have declared a temporary cease-fire from our normal sibling squabbling."

Mom, Dad, and Ethan burst out laughing. Ajax shouted, "What'd he say?"

Soon, Ethan and I were excused, but I stayed in the living room with my eyes on my book and my ears on the game. Mom and Dad worked with Matthew and Ajax for a long time.

"Here's a good one," Dad said. He shuffled to the door. When Ajax opened the door, Dad held out a gnarled hand.

"No!" Matthew shouted and ran from the room.

Mom ran after him, bringing him back in time to see Ajax say, "Hi, Rusty, nice bike."

Rusty is a homeless man who carries hedge clippers as he rides through town looking for work. Dad sometimes pays him to trim our hedges, then sits with him on the back porch while Rusty eats whatever food Mom gives him. Once she stirred real coffee in a mug of hot water, thinking it was instant coffee. That was the only thing Rusty ever refused.

"I don't have anything nice to say to him," Matthew yelled. "He's dirty."

"You'd be dirty too, if you didn't have a home," Mom said. She was probably trying to develop Matthew's compassion, but it backfired.

Matthew crossed his arms over his chest and glared, "That's why he smells so bad. He doesn't even have a bathroom."

Dad broke character and raised his eyebrows, looking pointedly at Matthew. Finally, Matthew said, "You're better at cutting hedges than Stephen. He gives them mohawks." Even though I was looking at my book, I knew Matthew was glaring at me, as if this whole game was my fault.

"That's better," Mom said.

"Really?" I asked, looking up from my book now.

"At least, a bit better," Dad added. "Okay, here's the last one. For tonight." Dad knocked on the front door again. Ajax opened the door. "¡Hola!" Dad said, pretending to be the neighbor who had just moved in next door. "Me llamo Señora Rodriguez," Dad said.

"That does it!" Ajax blew up. "I can't be polite in three languages!"

Mom threw her arms around Ajax. "Sure you can, kiddo!" We went to Colombia to adopt Matthew when he was four years old. We've all been learning Spanish ever since.

"¿Cómo está usted?" Ajax stuttered, with a terrible accent.

"¡Bravo! ¡Fantástico!" Dad yelled. "Give me five! That's my man! Polite in three languages! Now, you, Matthew."

"I hate talking Spanish," Matthew said.

"That's not polite in any language," Dad corrected.

"¿Cómo estás?" Dad asked.

"Bien. ¿Y usted?" Matthew said quietly.

Touché. Another victory for Dad.

CHAPTER 3

Bullies Foiled

Ajax

I WAS RACING MY car along the dining room table and twirling an airplane with my other hand. I was trying to push the car off the table and drop the airplane so they would crash on top of each other on the floor. I heard Stephen ask Mom if he could take the bus to the YMCA because he had left his foil at fencing class last night.

"Again?" Matthew laughed, but it wasn't a real laugh. Sort of a mean laugh.

"Can I go with him to get his sword?" I asked.

"Foil," Stephen said. "It's not a real sword—it's a fencing foil."

"I'll go, too," Ethan said. "So Stephen doesn't remember his foil and forget Ajax at the Y."

"I thought you wanted to fly that kite you've been making," Mom frowned at me. That was supposed to be my science lesson before I got more interested in running around with cars and airplanes, and Stephen told Mom he could turn that into a science lesson for me.

"Not much of a kite. Bet that ratty old thing won't even fly," Matthew said.

"Will too!" I yelled.

Ethan told Mom he would help me with my kite when we got home from the Y. "I'll make sure it'll fly," he whispered to me.

Mom gave Stephen enough money for the bus. Then she gave Ethan money, too. "This is enough to get there." Ethan put it in his pocket. "And this is enough to get home." Ethan put that in his other pocket. "In case Stephen loses his," she whispered. But I heard her. Because I'm like a superhero with supersonic ears.

After getting Stephen's sword, Ethan and Stephen and I played basketball. Then we waited for the bus. I took Stephen's sword and pretended to fight enemies. I bent my left arm and twirled the sword, moving up and down the sidewalk just like Stephen does at fencing class.

When the bus arrived, the driver said, "It's not every kid I'd let on my bus with a sword." He was kidding because he knows us.

"Actually, it's not a sword, just a foil," Stephen said. "So, you don't have to worry."

We were only halfway home when Ethan jabbed Stephen. He pointed out the window. I tried to stand up to see what they were looking at. Stephen pulled the cord so the bus driver would stop. Ethan grabbed my hand, and we ran off the bus. Stephen was already ahead of us. I'm superhero fast, but it was hard to keep up. Then I saw why we were running. Molly was lying on the sidewalk crying.

Kylie was looking wild. Two big boys had their backs to us. We could hear them yelling. "What's black and white and red all over?" One of the boys pulled Kylie's red hair.

"An ugly girl with a red rug head," the other boy sneered. The other boy kicked Molly and yelled, "Halfrican mutt."

The boys were laughing. Until they heard me shout in my superhero voice, "I'll teach you not to pick on little kids!" I got my fists ready, but Stephen put out his sword.

Ethan crouched by Molly, who kept wailing. Kylie ran behind me, then stuck out her tongue at the bullies.

The boys tried to run past us, but Stephen blocked them. "See this sword?" Stephen yelled, waving it madly. I couldn't believe my supersonic ears. He called it a sword. "Don't you pick on little kids again," he yelled. "Especially these two girls. Got it?" Stephen shook his sword at them again.

The boys backed up against the building and nodded their heads. Stephen let the boys go, but stood there watching them. They tried to walk off like they were cool. They looked back and saw Stephen still staring at them. Then they ran.

"Thanks, Stephen," Kylie laughed. "You were better than the lightnin' I prayed for."

"I thought it was a foil, not a sword," Ethan grinned.

"I was trying to make a point, and a sword—unlike a foil—has a point," Stephen said. He picked up Molly and handed me his sword.

Molly's knees were bloody so Stephen and Ethan took turns carrying her. Finally, we got to Molly and Kylie's house. Stephen explained what had happened to Molly and Kylie's grandma. She's Deaf, so Stephen was signing away.

Stephen asked Molly's grandma if he could use their phone to call Mom. "Their mom's at work, but they're okay," I heard Stephen tell Mom even though Molly was still crying.

Mom talked to Molly. Then she talked to Stephen again. I tried to practice fencing, but there was a play pen in the living room and toys all over the floor. I pretended I was a superhero spy and tried to figure out what Mom was saying from how Stephen answered. She must have told him to ask Molly's grandma if the girls could come to our house, because that's what he did. Even I could understand those easy signs.

"Isn't Dad home with the car yet?" Stephen groaned into the phone. "Do we have to walk more, ride more . . ." He looked at Molly, ". . . and cry more?"

After a pause, Stephen shook his head, "No, I spent all the money on the bus."

Ethan pulled out the just-in-case money Mom had given him and showed it to Stephen.

"Ethan has money—but just for three rides," Stephen told Mom.

Ethan pulled out the money from his other pocket. Stephen grinned, said good-bye, and hung up the phone.

Ethan helped Molly to the bus stop. Kylie bopped along, swinging my hand. Knights let little girls hold their hands. But not big girls.

"I want to plant a garden," Kylie said.

"Oh, so you can eat vegetables?" Ethan asked.

"No," Kylie laughed. "A rabbit will eat the vegetables. Then I can catch the rabbit."

The bus pulled up. "Well, silly rabbit, hop on!" Ethan said as Kylie jumped up the steps. Stephen carried Molly and plopped her, sort of crumpled, on his lap. We passed the billboard with a picture of a baby, and Kylie blew a kiss to the baby. When the woman behind her laughed, Kylie turned around and said, "Silly old giggler." If I had said that, Mom would have shushed me for sure. When we got off the bus, Kylie waved and everyone waved back.

Back at home, Stephen and Ethan helped me adjust the crossbow of my kite, while Mom cleaned up Molly's knees. Mom was giving her one of those talks—the kind where she asks a lot of questions but doesn't wait for answers. "Why were you two out alone? What were you doing? Did your mom know where you were?"

Molly answered, "Mama got a new job. She's at work."

Kylie said, "Grandma watched us but we snucked out 'cause we was lookin' for . . ." Molly jabbed Kylie. Usually Kylie would blow up about that, but she just shut up.

CHAPTER 4

Reeling in Matthew

Matthew

I CAN'T BELIEVE MOM let Stephen stay home but is making me go watch Ajax fly his dumb old kite. Stephen told her that he told Nikki—Pembrook and Janalia's big sister who lives across the street and is my age—that she could call him when she got home from school. He's going to help her with her report. Something about Marta Carla and a king who had to sign. We have to sign too—when Deaf people visit.

Mom told Stephen to make garlic bread to go with dinner. He asked a bunch of questions about what knife to use, how fat to cut the bread, and how much butter to put on. He wanted a recipe. Words get all tangled up in my head, but I know how to make garlic bread. Easy, peasy. Mom told him to pretend it was a math problem and figure it out. I hate math.

We walked up the street to the school. It has a great hill for sledding down in winter. Maybe if Ajax runs the whole way down the hill, his dumb old kite will stay up in the air a few seconds.

Mom, Molly, Kylie, and I sat on the grass. Ethan and Ajax came running down the hill. Ajax's kite flopped and fell. "I knew it," I said.

Mom gave me that sad look—the one that makes me feel like hiding. Ethan and Ajax knelt over the kite, moving the crossbar and fixing the tail. They started running again. A big wind blew, and Ajax's kite actually flew for a little while. He was smiling so big like he won a million dollars.

I saw Dad walking up to the school. "What are you doing here?" I asked when he sat down. He started on the manners talk again, but Molly and Kylie about attacked him with their crazy hugs and kisses. So I sneaked off without a talking-to.

Molly and Kylie followed me, and Molly started in on me. "Please, please, please," Molly kept saying. "Come with us to the Lion Man's house." I told her she was crazy, and I didn't care about those dumb lions for Ajax.

Kylie got all braggy, "Well, we're going to the Lion Man's. You don't have to come. We can do it ourselves."

"Please." Molly looked like she was going to cry. She was making me feel icky. Like there was something hot and gooey sticking to me. Like I wanted to scrape it off with a fork, but the fork would get stuck, and I'd have to use a shovel. But the shovel would get stuck, and I'd be clanging around with a fork and shovel, which would make people look at me funny, which would make it all worse.

"All right," I agreed, which took away some of the hot, sticky feeling. "But, I won't talk to him."

"What will you do if he does eat kids?" Kylie asked.

"Don't be dumb. No one eats kids," I told her. Then I added, "I'd get the police." I heard Dad's cell phone ringing. That gave me an idea. "When we go, I'll take Dad's phone. If the man tries to hurt you, I'll call the police."

"We can give the lions for Ajax's birthday!" Kylie said.

"When is his birthday?" Molly looked worried.

"May 16," I said.

"When's that?" asked Kylie. She hardly knows anything.

"Soon, maybe two weeks."

"How will we pay for the lions?" Molly wondered.

"We could sell our baby sister," Kylie said.

"That's against the law," I said. Little kids have dumb ideas.

"Too bad," Kylie said, shaking her head.

"Besides, who would buy MaKayla?" I added.

"Do you have any money?" Molly asked.

"Not for lions for Ajax. I need my money," I told her.

"What for?" Kylie asked.

"For important things," I tried not to look at Molly.

They both said, "Like what?" They were really ganging up on me.

"Like things that aren't lions for Ajax," I told them.

"I know," said Molly, "we can put our toys in a wagon, and pull it down the street and sell them. Like the yard sale Mama had last year, only moving."

I can't think of anyone who would buy their dumb old toys, but if I said that they'd go right back to asking me for money. Right then, Mom told Ajax to reel in his kite and called all of us to start walking home. That made Molly and Kylie shut up about the money.

As we walked home, Dad kept praising Ajax like he was some kind of hero, "Champion of the uncharted skies!" Mom told Dad all about Stephen not knowing how to make garlic bread.

"Oh, don't worry about Stephen," Dad said. "When I got home from work, he told me I'd find you all up here. He was talking to Nikki on the phone, saying he would tell her everything he knew about King John signing the Magna Carta if she would tell him everything she knew about making garlic bread."

"Poor Nikki," Mom said. "She doesn't have any idea how little Stephen knows about making garlic bread."

"Or how much he knows about history," added Ethan.

CHAPTER 5

Gotcha Day

Ethan

WE WERE HAVING A party because it was Matthew's Gotcha Day. It had been exactly five years since we had met him in Colombia. Matthew, Ajax, Molly, and Kylie were playing in the backyard. The rest of us were making Matthew's favorite dinner. At least, Mom and Dad and I were. Stephen was talking about quasars and pulsars. He usually gets bored doing one thing at a time. He plays clarinet while he reads physics books and shoots hoops while we practice Spanish. Yes, we have a small backboard in our bedroom since our real one keeps getting stolen from our backyard. When it comes to anything practical though—like setting the table—he stops working when he starts talking, which is most of the time.

So, I was grabbing the silverware to set the table—Stephen's job—when I noticed Molly just standing at the back door. I opened the kitchen door and yelled, "Look who I found!"

Molly hung her head, "I couldn't open the door."

"Just ask, silly girl!" I ruffled her curly brown hair.

"I didn't want to bother anyone," she said, twisting her hands.

Dad scooped her up in his arms and laughed, "You're a buddy, not a bother." He set her down and turned back to the hamburgers he was cooking.

Mom looked up from the salad she was making and asked me to help Molly put balloons all over the dining room. I took Molly into the dining room and gave her the clump of balloon strings.

While I finished setting the table, Molly walked around

the dining room releasing one balloon after another. When I came back to the kitchen to get the French fries, there was a pounding on the back door. Kylie shouted over the pounding, "Joey!" No one but Kylie gets away with calling my dad Joey. "Joey! Open the door!" Dad opened the door just a crack.

"Please," Kylie added. Not even Kylie gets away with barking out orders and not saying please. She leaped into Dad's arms, then hopped down and pranced into the dining room. "Balloons!" Kylie exclaimed. "Balloons swimming in the sky!"

It took a bit of doing on Mom and Dad's part, but finally all eight of us were sitting at the dining room table. We were having Matthew's favorite meal, cheeseburgers and French fries, plus Mom's Mandatory Salad—that's actually what we call it because she makes us eat as many bites of it as our age. That's thirteen bites for Stephen, eleven for me, nine bites for Matthew, six for Ajax and Molly, and five for Kylie.

"I have an idea!" Mom exclaimed. Stephen and I looked at each other. Dad says we are not allowed to groan when Mom proclaims an idea, which she does about a dozen times a day. "Let's all take turns praying, thanking God for Matthew."

"I'll start," Kylie piped up. "Thank you, God, for Matthew— that he draws pictures for me. She turned to Matthew and added, "After dinner, will you draw a red bike for me? And a dinosaur? And my dog?"

Dad turned to Molly and asked if she wanted to pray. "Thank you, God, that Matthew teaches me how to dance," mumbled Molly. Dad squeezed her hand and looked at Ajax.

"Thank you, God, that Matthew doesn't share a room with me anymore," prayed Ajax.

My turn. "Thank you, God, that Matthew joined our family five years ago, and thank you that Matthew helped me talk Mom and Dad into getting a dog," I said, petting Fluffernutter. I had named the tan and white mutt we had gotten from the SPCA after peanut butter and marshmallow sandwiches, which I used to like (but can't stand now).

Mom and Dad almost changed their minds about getting Fluffer when the SPCA people kept asking which dog we wanted to adopt. "Adoption is permanent," Dad had told the SPCA people. When he noticed Fluffer gnawing at my arm, he added, "And if this dog ruins my computer by chewing through the cord—like Matthew ruined my computer by spilling lemonade on it—the dog, unlike Matthew, will not have a permanent home."

Good thing there were so many dogs barking that the SPCA volunteer didn't hear Dad. Then Mom and Dad almost backed out when it came time to sign the papers. They complained that they had to give up more rights to take home a dog than to adopt a child. Mom and Dad talked about that the whole ride home, saying that they didn't have to let Ajax and Matthew's adoption agencies know if we moved or allow their social workers to enter our home any time, unannounced, to see how they were caring for the kids.

I think Mom and Dad would have walked out without Fluffer if not for those social workers. Matthew has what they call "attachment issues," among other things—many other things. The social workers thought it might be easier for him to trust a dog than us. So, thanks to the social workers, we got a dog, and—sure enough—Matthew had gotten what he had called his first friend: Fluffernutter. Emphasis on had called. One day Matthew was running around the house with dozens of bells pinned to his pajamas. Fluffer growled at him, and that was the end of their friendship. "Friends don't growl at each other," Matthew said. "I kicked Fluffer out of my world." Still, it's thanks to Matthew that I got Fluffer.

Meanwhile, Stephen was praying. "Thank you, God, that Matthew came to us, since he taught me that faith is knowing there is gravity, even though birds can fly." Stephen likes to talk in riddles.

"Father, thank you that Matthew has lived up to his name and has truly been a wonderful gift from you," Mom prayed.

"Thank you, Father, for Matthew," Dad began. "Thank you that he belongs in this family. We pray that you would root him deep in Jesus, so he can be filled with joy."

Dinner was our usual free-for-all of talking and teasing. Then we had the cake that Matthew had made—with Mom's supervision, of course. I'm the only kid in the family who is allowed to use the oven or the stove without Mom supervising. She thinks the other kids would end up playing sports in the living room (that would be Ajax), doing art at the dining room table (that would be Matthew), or reading (that would be Stephen), and burning the house down. She's probably right. Matthew had made a Funfetti cake and slathered it with sprinkles. Seriously, there were so many sprinkles on the cake that we had to crunch through the icing.

After dinner, we went to the living room, where Mom had hidden a present for each of us. "How come everyone gets a present when it's my Gotcha Day?" Matthew demanded.

"Well, since you and Ajax have birthday celebrations and Gotcha Day parties, but Stephen and Ethan only have birthdays, we like to give everyone a gift on your Adoption Day," Mom explained with a sigh.

"You don't like me," Matthew scowled.

"I love you, Matthew. It's just that I have explained this to you ten times already today."

"And thirteen times yesterday," Stephen said.

"And sixteen times the day before," I added.

"And sixty-three times before that," Ajax jumped in.

"That makes one hundred and three explanations," Stephen concluded.

"One hundred two," I corrected.

"One hundred three," Stephen maintained, "You forgot the explanation Mom gave just now, before the ten others today, the thirteen yesterday, the sixteen . . ." I should have known better than to correct Stephen's math.

"Well, maybe we should forget about the presents," Dad teased.

"No way!" Ajax shouted.

Kylie found a package with her name. She tore open the wrapping and hugged the cloth doll. Mom explained that the doll was wearing a traditional Colombian costume—a green and red striped skirt and a red cape with green stars.

"She's supposed to be wearing a traditional Colombian costume," Stephen began. "But it's all wrong."

"Since when do you know about skirts?" Matthew sneered.

"Since we got stuck in Bogotá waiting for your adoption papers and visited every museum in the city—including the Regional Costume Museum," Stephen retorted. "So, I know, for example, that this girl's cape is called a ruana."

"Her ruana is the color of the flag of Boyacá," I offered.

Mom's mouth was hanging open. "How can you remember

all this? You were so little when we were in Colombia," she exclaimed.

"Remember that soccer ball I got in Colombia?" I replied. "It's decorated with the names and flags of all the states of Colombia."

"Actually," Stephen corrected, "they're not states, they're departments. And we saw a lot of ruanas, but none with stars," he added. "We saw a lot of flouncy skirts like this, but always with flouncy blouses—never with a ruana."

"Those flouncy skirts are called polleras," Dad said.

Mom just looked at us, amazed. So did Matthew, who mumbled, "I thought I was the only boy in this family who liked skirts."

"Well," Mom turned back to Kylie and hurried to change the subject. "It seems your doll is wearing more of a Christmas costume than a Colombian costume."

"Then I'll call her Nabeeda!" Kylie shouted triumphantly.

"Nabeeda?" Stephen exploded.

"Yep," Kylie cuddled her doll. "'Cause I can talk Spanish. And she's wearing Christmas colors."

"Nabeeda for Christmas colors?" I asked.

"If you went to A B C D Good School, you'd know."

"Would know what?" I pursued.

"We singed it at Christmas," Kylie said.

"Oh, feliz navidad." I finally got it. "Navidad," I said slowly.

"That's what I said. Nabeeda. I'll take her to school with me tomorrow. And I won't let Buster eat her up. Buster eats stuffs—like cereal boxes and backpacks and everything we leave on the floor. "

"Would he eat MaKayla if you left her . . .?" Matthew began. Dad gave him that look, and Matthew shut up.

Molly also got a Latin American doll, but hers had light brown hair that hung in ringlets, just like Molly's own hair. Mom said she had tried to find a doll with curly red hair for Kylie, but red-haired Colombian dolls are hard to come by. Molly's doll wore a jumper with llamas woven into the fabric. "What's a good name for my doll?" Molly asked.

"Anything you want," Dad answered.

"Something pretty, like Delilah," Matthew suggested. We all groaned. When Mom and Dad had finished reading a children's Bible to Matthew and Ajax recently, Matthew announced, "I like Delilah best of all."

"How 'bout Polly?" Molly asked, looking down at her doll. "I always wanted a sister who rhymed with me."

"That's great," I said. "Maybe at Christmas you can get a Holly doll."

"And a Collie doll," added Ajax.

"That's a dog," said Matthew disgustedly.

"What about Folly?" Stephen asked.

"Or Golly?" Dad jumped in. "Golly's middle initial could be G, and her last name could be Willikers." We stared at Dad, who explained. "People used to say, 'Golly gee willikers,' like in, 'Golly gee willikers, that's so funny.'"

"Or a doll named Lolly, with the last name Pop?" I added.

"Or Volley, with the last name Ball," Ajax joined in.

"All right, guys," Dad said, taking Molly onto his lap. "Polly is a sweet name for your doll. Almost as sweet as you are."

Ajax's gift was wrapped in bright paper that was covered with rain forest scenes. He tore open the paper to find a stuffed toucan. "Thanks, Mom and Dad!" Ajax yelled. "I needed one more player for my stuffed animal football teams. Will you play another game of stuffed animal football with me?" Ajax asked, turning to me.

When I nodded, Ajax shouted, "Yippee!"

"She's pretty," Molly said, reaching her hand toward the toucan.

"He's a football player," Ajax corrected. Then, seeing Molly's eyes droop, he added, "He's not playing football now. Want to hold him?"

Dad handed Matthew his present, which was a small box wrapped in shiny gold paper.

"I love that paper," Matthew said.

"I knew you would," Dad replied. "That's why I sneaked it into the cart when you were looking at fabric paints." Dad does most of the shopping because he usually has the car, and because Mom goes crazy trying to shop with Matthew and Ajax along.

"Why is it so small?" Matthew asked.

"Good things come in small packages," Dad said. "Like you," he added, reaching out to tousle Matthew's hair.

Matthew turned away, yelling, "I'm big now!"

"Well, open it," Dad sighed. He never used to sigh.

Matthew carefully removed the wrapping paper and opened the box. "Tickets?" he asked.

"To see Ballet Folklórico—a Mexican dance company— where men use their strength," Dad picked up Mom and whirled her in the air, "to show the beauty of women."

"Humph," Matthew snorted. "I hope they dance better than you two."

"It will be showing downtown at the Strand Theatre," Mom laughed as Dad plunked her back on the floor. "Not 'til fall, but you've always wanted to go there."

"I don't just want to go there. I want to own it," Matthew said.

"Matthew," Dad had reached his limit. "You love dance. You love music. This gift has both, and it's at a place you've begged us to take you."

I started opening my gift, hoping to break up the tension. It was several sets of Latin American stamps. Because I am the only child in the Trellert family who can sit still long enough to work on a stamp collection, I inherited my grandfather's stamp books. "Wow, thanks," I said with more enthusiasm than I felt.

Mom nudged Stephen, who was reading a book, "What are you reading now?"

"*Mathematics without Pragmatics,*" Stephen answered. "Math is so cool without all those numbers. Until you get to higher math, everything has numbers, but now I can do all sorts of math without messing with numbers."

"Well, open your present," Mom said. Sometimes we don't have a clue how to respond to Stephen's comments.

"Oh, thanks!" Stephen said, opening his package to find— what else?—a book.

"What is it?" Ajax asked.

"*Game Theory,*" Mom responded, since Stephen was already reading the new book.

"I like games!" Ajax said.

"Not these kinds of games," Stephen said looking up from his book. "This was written by a Colombian mathematician."

"I need a math magician," Molly whispered to me. "I get bad grades in math."

"You've heard of this guy?" Mom questioned. "Do you know how many phone calls I made before I tracked down a book written by a Colombian mathematician?"

"Internet, Mom. It should be every homeschool mom's best friend," Stephen said. "There are plenty of Colombian mathematicians." He actually began rattling off names, but Kylie interrupted him.

"Now, let's play Doggy and Owner," Kylie laughed. "Matthew, you can be my doggy." Kylie dragged Matthew by his shirt collar.

I couldn't believe Matthew went along with her, but he just groaned, "I'd rather have Molly be my owner."

"Okay," Kylie pushed Matthew over to Molly. "Ajax, you be my dog. Ajax is a good name for a dog, just like Nabeeda is a good name for a doll. Now, don't you eat my doll, Ajax," said Kylie, smacking Ajax on the head.

Ajax yelped, sounding like a hurt dog. I tried, "Kylie, be nice to your dog, like this." I patted Ajax on the head.

"No," Kylie yelled, this time hitting Ajax with her doll. That's when Dad stepped in. He took Nabeeda from Kylie. Now it was Kylie's turn to yelp. "He's a bad doggy. He eats peoples," Kylie protested. "And it's my doll!"

"I didn't give you this doll so you could whack people with it," Dad explained.

Kylie argued, "But he's a . . ."

Dad overruled, of course. "I didn't give you this so you could whack people or pretend dogs with it."

Kylie backed down, but Dad held on to Nabeeda. "Sorry," Kylie patted Ajax on the head. Dad kept his grip on the doll and his eyes on Kylie. "Please forgive me for being mean," Kylie said.

Dad grinned at Kylie and gave her the doll. Kylie sat on Mom's lap, cuddling Nabeeda.

Mom had gotten out the scrapbook that has the only bits we have from Matthew's first four years in Colombia. She opened it to the first page, which has the only baby picture we have of Matthew. The orphanage had sent it after we applied to adopt him. Matthew threw his hands over the photo and yelled, "I hate that picture. I look so ugly."

"Matthew," Mom began, "I love looking at this book and

seeing all the photos of when we first met you. See, these are pictures of people at the orphanage who took care of you." She flipped ahead a few pages and pointed to some other photos. "I love seeing all the beautiful buildings, flowers, and people of Colombia." Mom pointed to a picture of Matthew in a tropical garden as she went on, "Most of all, I love seeing you and remembering what a wonderful child you were."

"I hate this book," Matthew said.

Mom sighed and put the scrapbook away. Dad told the girls it was time to head home and told Stephen and me to start on the dishes. Mom took Stephen's new book out of his hands.

"Were you talking to me?" Stephen asked.

"Yes, say good-bye to the girls, then come help with the dishes," Mom explained.

"See you, Molly," Stephen scooped up Molly. "Take good care of Polly," Stephen added as he passed her to me. Just in time—a second before Kylie flew into Stephen's lap.

I held Molly on my lap. She pointed up at the balloons and looked at me questioningly. "Would you like to take a balloon home with you?" I asked. Molly nodded her head.

"Those are my balloons, from my party," Matthew yelled.

We all looked at Matthew. "Of course she can—right, Matthew?" Stephen said. Somehow Stephen can work magic with Matthew, even though they have nothing in common.

"All right," Matthew growled. "Molly can take home one balloon. One."

Molly kissed the toucan and set it on the dining room table. She and Polly picked a pink balloon.

Stephen passed Kylie to me. "And one for Kylie?" I questioned, hoping some of Stephen's magic would rub off on me.

Matthew frowned, but didn't say anything as Kylie hopped off my lap, pulled me into the dining room, and pointed out two balloons. "I want that green one. Over there." Kylie jumped up and down while she added, "And, I want a red one for Nabeeda, too. Can I have one for Nabeeda, Matthew?"

Matthew sighed.

"And can Molly take one home for Polly, too?" Kylie asked, jumping up and down.

"Okay, then no more questions!" Matthew roared.

CHAPTER 6

Thanks for the Tickets

Stephen

MATTHEW'S GOTCHA DAY PARTY was over. Dad was back home getting Ajax into bed. At least that was Dad's goal, but, of course, not Ajax's. I could hear his protests because his bedroom is next to the one that Ethan and I share. "No stuffy football?" Ajax whined.

"Tomorrow!" Ethan shouted from the top bunk of our bed.

Ajax asked, "How old is Kylie?"

"Kylie is five," Dad answered. "Now, lie down."

I heard the wallop of Ajax thumping himself down on his bed, but he didn't turn down the energy or the volume. "And, how old is MaKayla?"

Dad answered, "She just turned two. Only one more question."

"Can I ask two more?"

"Yes, but that was one of them," Dad laughed. "Now, only one more."

"Molly and me are six, but I'll be seven soon."

"Right, now let's pray."

"But, that wasn't a question. So, my last question is, 'Would you send Mom in so she can answer a few more questions?'"

"You sure drive a hard bargain," Dad chuckled. "All right, Ajax, after we pray."

When Mom came into his room, Ajax still had his usual volume cranked, "Why does Molly and Kylie's little sister have such a funny name?"

"Most people would think you have a funny name, Ajax," Mom began. She was talking in her teacher voice, which made it easy to hear her, too. "Well, their mom's name is Missy. Really, her name is Michelle, but she's always been called Missy."

"Why?" Ajax interrupted.

"I don't know," Mom answered. "She wanted Molly's name to begin with an M, like her name. Then Kylie's dad . . ."

"Kylie doesn't have a dad," Ajax interrupted.

"She has a dad. Everyone does," Mom explained. "But, her dad doesn't live with them."

"That's bad," Ajax said.

"Well," Mom began. "It's sad for those girls to grow up without a dad, but, Kylie's dad wasn't very nice."

"Why?" Ajax asked.

"NFK," Mom said.

NFK means not for kids, and it is one of Ajax's least favorite terms. "If I met him, I'd show him a thing or two!" Ajax shouted. Then he added, "So Molly has a dad, too?"

"Yes, Molly has a dad, but he never did live with them."

"Why not?"

"Well, Ajax, you know that's not God's plan," Mom hedged.

"I know, 'One man, one woman, husband and wife for the rest of their life,'" Ajax repeated the mantra we had all heard hundreds of times.

"So, why does Molly and Kylie's sister have such a funny name?"

"Oh yeah," Mom continued. "Kylie's dad wanted her name to start with a K, like his."

"What was his name?" Ajax interrupted.

"Kevin," Mom went on, "Then Missy and Kevin were expecting another baby. They decided to make sure that child's name had a capital M and a capital K in it."

"Names can only have one capital letter. Ethan taught me that when he showed me how to write my name," Ajax said proudly.

"Well, some names only have one capital letter, but lots of names now have two. MaKayla has a capital M, then a small 'a' then a capital K."

"Oh. How did we meet Molly and Kylie?" Ajax went on.

"Well, Missy was having a lot of trouble," Mom began.

"What kind of trouble?" Ajax wanted to know.

"NFK."

"All the good stuff is NFK," Ajax complained.

"No, all the bad stuff is NFK," Mom corrected. "Missy used to live down the street."

"They sure move a lot," Ajax said.

Mom went on, "The girls stayed with us when their mom was . . . away for a while. Now, no more questions about that. And I think you would hurt the girls' feelings if you talked to them about their dads, so please don't bring it up."

"Okay. Now I know how they got their names. How did Stephen get his name?"

"When I was pregnant with Stephen, Dad and I were studying the book of Acts, in the Bible. Stephen loved Jesus, and people killed him because of it. We prayed for our little baby to love God like Stephen did . . ."

"He was just a baby and you wanted him to get killed?" Ajax exploded.

"No," Mom laughed, "we just wanted him to love Jesus that much. Stephen means 'crown.' Do you know what Stephen's middle name is?"

"It's Joseph," Ajax answered.

"Yep. And Joseph means, 'He shall add.' So Stephen Joseph means, 'He shall add crowns.' That's funny, because we had already planned to give him that name. Then—when he was born—we saw that he had two crowns on his head."

"He was born with crowns on his head?" Ajax burst out.

"Not king's crowns, but if you look at his head you can see . . ."

Ajax barged into my room, where he grabbed my head and pushed it down into my book. Math off; Ajax on. He rummaged through my hair with his fingers.

"Ow," I groaned.

"Here, let me show you," Ethan jumped down from the top bunk. "See, Ajax, they're circles," Ethan showed him, helping Ajax trace the crowns with his finger.

"Now, to bed, Ajax," Mom commanded, walking into our room.

"Is that why Stephen's hair always sticks up in the back?" Ajax asked as he and Mom walked out of the room.

I retorted, "No, Ajax, it's because all my brain power pushes my hair up there. Close the door and remember a closed door isn't an open invitation. It's a reminder to knock."

"Now, last question," Mom said.

"How did Ethan get his name?" Ajax asked.

"Ethan is mentioned in the Bible as a man who sang praises to God. Your Dad and I were learning about worship while I was pregnant with Ethan. In fact, Dad was teaching a class on worship at the Deaf church. So, we prayed that our baby would love to worship God, and we named him Ethan. Now, that's it."

"Okay, just one bedtime story," Ajax said.

"A story?" Now it was Mom's turn to explode.

"Yeah, about how I got my name."

"All right," Mom quickly told the story that we all knew by heart. "Your birth mother named you Wrex."

"Like someone who wrecks a lot of cars?" Ajax asked.

"No, W-r-e-x," Mom spelled.

"Wrex starts with a W?" Ajax asked incredulously.

Mom explained. "Just like the word write: w-r-i-t-e. Write begins with a 'w' that you can't hear. We call that a silent letter. Anyhow, your foster parents never called you Wrex."

"What did they call me?" Ajax wondered.

"I don't know what they called you at first, but the first food you ate was Apple Jacks cereal."

"They gave me Apple Jacks for breakfast? You never let us eat junky cereals. If I still lived with them, could I still eat Apple Jacks?" Ajax asked.

"Anyhow," Mom went on, resolving to finish, "they called you Apple Jacks. When we met you, you said, 'Hi, I Apple Jacks.' We didn't want to take away your name, but we hardly wanted to call you the name of some cereal we didn't want you to eat."

"Why can't I eat it?" Ajax asked.

"Because it's expensive, and it's not good for you." Mom's voice was getting strained. "So, we gradually changed your nickname to Ajax, then picked your name, Aaron Gyasi, to fit your nickname—at least, sort of. Although, the way you went running into Stephen and Ethan's room, I'm ready to change your nickname from Ajax to Comet."

"What do you mean?" asked Ajax.

"Ajax and Comet are the names of two cleaning powders," Mom sighed. She had set herself up for this one. "A comet goes racing around the world with a tail of fire."

"I'd like to be called Comet. Now, what about Matthew's name?"

"Absolutely not!" Mom said in her strictest voice. "You need your sleep. We can talk about Matthew's name tomorrow."

"Okay." Then Ajax added, "Mom, when are you going to start teaching me?"

"When you start sitting still for more than a minute. No more questions, little man." Mom said. "Good night."

"Oh boy," Mom came into our room—forgetting to knock, again—and sank down at the big desk Ethan and I share, pulling out our Spanish journals. "Ajax wants to know when I'm going to start teaching him. I'm going to have to cram that into my days next fall."

I looked up from my book. "You're already teaching him, Mom. Tonight you covered capital and lowercase letters when you explained the girls' names. You went on to social skills when you told him not to talk to them about their dads, and touched on some Greek and Hebrew when you explained our names. Not to mention, Bible and church history. When he looked at the crowns on my head, he learned about physiology and basic shapes. That lesson on the silent 'w' was rather advanced. You addressed nutrition with the lecture against junk cereals. You could have covered economics better by comparing the price of oatmeal with Apple Jacks. And the bit about comets was a science tidbit. You missed your chance on chemistry, though. You could have explained that we don't use those cleaning powders because they're abrasive. Still, I'd call that a good school day for a kid who never sits still."

"Plus, he learned a bit about Colombia from Matthew's scrapbook and our gifts," Ethan added.

Just then, Matthew barged in without so much as a knock, of course, and slammed the door behind him. "What are you doing out of bed?" Mom asked.

"I want to go see that play at the Strand," Matthew said.

"Oh?" Mom raised her eyebrows.

"Yeah, thanks for the tickets," Matthew mumbled.

Dad used the basket of dirty clothes in his arms to push open our door—without knocking, just like everyone else in the family. "Did you hear that?" Mom looked at Dad.

"Sure did. Thank you, Matthew. We'll look forward to going to that play with you. Now, off to bed, big buddy. You were so kind to share your balloons with Molly and Kylie."

"I hate when you talk like that." Matthew spun around and ran to the stairs leading up to his bedroom on the third floor.

"What did I do wrong now?" Dad signed to Mom.

"But, he thanked us, without being forced. That's the first time he's ever done that," Mom signed back.

Sometimes they forget that Ethan and I can understand everything they sign to each other.

CHAPTER 7

Cockroach or Superhero

Matthew

AJAX, ETHAN, STEPHEN, MOM, and I walked out of Martin Library. Each of us had a stack of books to carry. Ajax carried all the biggest and heaviest books—Stephen's books. Ajax could barely see over his stack. "Big is my specialty!" he boasted.

"Music!" I shouted. Ajax talks about his supersonic ears, but I'm the one who hears everything. I headed in the direction of the music.

"Whoa!" Mom shouted.

"Can't we go?" Ajax asked. For once, we were on the same side.

"It's the Box Lunch Revue," Stephen said.

"At Cherry Lane," Ethan added. It seemed like even Ethan and Stephen were on my side. They play in the band at Smith Middle School because Mom can't teach us music. She can't even sing. Last year, the school band played at Cherry Lane. Stephen was in the band, but not Ethan because he wasn't in middle school then. We had to go hear Stephen play, even though it rained and the music was stupid.

Mom looked at her watch. Dad was working at home today, so it was her turn to use the car. She could have taken us some place cool, like the mall. But she took us to the library. "Let's see." Mom talks to herself when she has to decide things. "I don't want to fight for another parking space. How long will it take us to walk there?" she asked.

"It's quick," I said, pointing down the street. "You go toward the one with old toys, not the one with the old shops and picture blankets. You pass the white building with the printed doors and the painted ceiling. Then you pass the wavy building with silver stripes. Go by the hotel with the red and pink flowers and the people looking at us sitting at tables. You pass the lion at the big building with pillars, and the little building with pillars on the other side. You pass the little building with white shutters and the stone stair that doesn't go anywhere but says MEN. You pass the trolley man stand and the building with the triangle tops, and there you are. It's across the street from the church with the tall, medium, and short triangles."

Mom looked confused. She's not very good at finding places.

Stephen said, "He's right." I don't think he's ever said that before. Stephen went on, "He means that you walk west on Market Street, toward the Bonham House—remember it has old toys?—not toward the York County Heritage Trust, which has that room showing an old-fashioned street of shops. The picture blankets are the old quilts displayed there. You pass the York Water Company. Its doors are embossed or something—like relief sculpture. Remember we went in there on New Year's Eve and saw the painted ceiling?"

"First Night," Mom said. "Go on."

"The wavy building with silver stripes is the AAA building," Stephen explained.

"The Art Deco building," Mom said.

"The hotel is the Yorktowne. It must have flowers," Stephen went on.

"Duh," I said.

"And the people aren't looking at us sitting at tables. He means that people sitting at tables by the window look out at us when we walk by."

"Like I said," I added.

"The big building with pillars is the courthouse," Ethan said, catching on. "It has a lion fountain." He can be a little slow. "The little building with pillars is the York Trust Company, across the street from it. The little building with the white shutters is . . . ."

"The Golden Swan," Stephen butted in.

Mom was frowning. "I've lived in this city for years. I have no idea what stairway he's talking about."

Stephen said, "There is a stairway that goes down there. The walls and railing around it are stone. We'll show you."

Ethan added, "The stairs must have gone to a men's room before, but—Matthew's right—they don't seem to go anywhere now because it's chained.

Wow! All my brothers fighting to do what I want, and two of them saying I'm right!

"There's a sign there," Ethan explained, "saying the old courthouse was there, when they wrote the . . ." Something or other. Sometimes Ethan uses big words like Stephen.

Mom shook her head, "You're amazing, Matthew. Sure," she decided. "Let's put these books in the car. Then we can walk down. I want to see all these places through your eyes, Matthew."

Don't ask me how she's going to do that, but I'm not going to argue. After we passed the buildings with pillars, Mom looked from one side of the street to the other. "There's the funny trolley man stand," I pointed.

"The trolley kiosk," Stephen said, like Mr. Know-it-all.

I pointed across the street. "There's the building with triangle tops."

Mom said, "How could I have missed how beautiful that building is?"

Ethan asked, "What do you call those things on top of it?"

"Triangles," I said.

Stephen—like a know-it-all again—said, "Tetrahedrons."

"That's a dumb name." I said.

Mom started in with her teacher voice, "Tetrahedrons. It means . . ."

"Pyramid spires?" Ethan asked.

"Triangles," I said.

Mom made us cross the street. We looked down the stone stairway even though it doesn't go anywhere. Then we crossed the road again. As we walked toward the music, Stephen pointed to a church and asked Mom, "See the tall, medium, and small triangles?"

Just like I said.

Mom said the place with the music is Cherry Lane and it doesn't always have music, only some days at lunchtime in the spring and summer. We found seats on an empty bench near the jazz band. Ajax went up to some boy who was holding a Nerf ball. The two of them tossed the ball back and forth. Suddenly, an old lady popped up from the bench near the trumpet player and started dancing. The lady's purple high heels clicked on the cement. She wore a black and gold skirt that shimmered in the sun. Her blue-like-the-sky blouse, with its puffy sleeves, waved in the breeze. On top of her white hair was an orange beret with sequins.

Stephen whispered to Mom, "She looks like one of Matthew's drawings come to life."

I didn't know if that was good or bad, so I glared at him just in case.

The old woman kept dancing. A man with a flag bandana on his head threw his cigarette on the ground and edged away from the woman. I said, "She can't dance."

Mom hissed, "Hush. I know that woman. That's the great thing about living here in York. You can get to know the colorful characters."

"She is colorful," I whispered back. "But she's not in a book, and she still can't dance."

"She lives across the street from the city health clinic," Mom whispered. "When Dad and I went there to get our tetanus shots, she was sitting on the stoop beside our parking spot. She told us to say hello to the nurses in the clinic. When we did, they rolled their eyes—like you just did." She gave me that look. "But when we went back to the car, she asked if we gave the nurses her message. Dad said, 'Oh, yes, and they love you too.'"

"He lied," I glared. Then I added, "What's her name?"

"Phoebe," Mom answered.

The music stopped, but Phoebe kept right on dancing. Stephen asked if he could run ahead of us back to the library. He remembered that he forgot a whole stack of books on the table there. He forgets everything. Mom gave him her library card and told him to hurry. She told him to stay at the library until we got back to the car. Then she shouted after him, "See if you can get a book on York's art and texture."

"Why do you want a book about art and texture?" I asked. It sounded like she was planning some art projects for me. But

I like to plan my own art projects.

"To learn about the building with the triangle tops," Mom explained. Then she looked at me and said, 'Ark-i-tek-ture.' It means the study of buildings. Maybe it's something you should learn about. We could do an ark-i-tek-ture treasure hunt downtown. All the things you notice have names," Mom said as we walked through the alley back toward our car.

Mom was on her worst kind of idea-go-round—the teacher kind. "We could start with the—did you ever notice?" She turned to me. "Oh, of course you did. We could start with the Florentine dome on the courthouse. What did he call that?" Now she turned to Ethan.

"The big building with the pillars," Ethan answered.

"Right," Mom said. There was no stopping her now. "That has Florentine domes."

I heard shouting up ahead, but Mom didn't seem to notice. She just kept talking, "We'd have to include the Golden Plough, with its half-timber style."

As the noise got louder, I grabbed Mom's hand and pointed. Mom dropped my hand and ran toward two shouting boys. Their backs were to us, but I heard bits of what they were saying, "Velcrohead . . . ketchup hair." In my head, I was drawing a picture of a kid with Velcro eyebrows that looped over like shoe straps and long blonde hair streaked with ketchup.

Mom shouted and the boys spun around. Now I could see who they were calling "ketchup hair." Kylie. Molly and Kylie were on the pavement, beside a wagon filled with their junky toys. Ethan picked up Molly, who was bawling. Mom bent over the two boys, holding their arms. Mom looked into the eyes of one boy, then the other. I've been on the other side of Mom's mad and sad look. Those boys didn't like it any more than me. The two boys tried to pull away from her, but Mom held on to them.

"Hey, you can't do this to me!" the taller boy began.

"Yeah, we'll call the cops," the smaller boy added.

"Please do," Mom said. That shut them up.

Mom kept looking at them. Her eyes went soft, but her hands stayed hard. The boys began to make excuses. "We was just playin'," the taller boy said.

"We didn't mean nothin'," the other boy said. He kicked at the pebbles in the alley.

"We was just havin' fun," the taller boy mumbled.

Mom isn't big on excuses. They hung their heads. Finally, Mom said, "Would you rather be like a cockroach or like a superhero?"

The boys looked at Mom. She explained, "When a superhero sees people who are weaker than he is, he helps them. He's a hero. But roaches are cannibals. When they see something weaker than themselves, they destroy it." Mom asked the taller boy, "What's your name?"

"Cody," the boy mumbled.

"And yours?" Mom asked the other boy.

"Brandon," he answered.

"Cody and Brandon," Mom began, "is there anything you want to say?"

"Sorry," Cody said quietly.

"Me too," Brandon almost whispered.

"Good. I hope the girls will forgive you." Mom looked at Kylie when she said this. As the two boys turned to leave, Mom added, "Boys, wouldn't it be fun to be a superhero?"

Cody and Brandon looked at Mom, then ran away.

Ethan set Molly down and Mom hugged the girls. We walked back toward the car. Molly dragged the wagon behind her.

Then Mom let the girls have it, "You can't keep on wandering around the city alone!"

"They're not alone," I said, "they're together."

Mom didn't pay any attention to me. "You're both too young to be walking around the city. What were you doing here? And why are you dragging this wagon around?"

"We're selling toys 'cause we need money," Kylie said. Molly jabbed Kylie and put her finger to her lips.

"They always need money," Ajax said.

Mom sighed. She didn't ask any more questions. She just shook her head and helped Molly pull the wagon.

Ajax said, "I didn't know roaches ate each other."

"That's cool," I said. "I'd like to see that."

It took a while, but we finally made it back to the car. Mom even remembered to send Ethan into the library for Stephen.

We were all bunched up with six kids and the wagon. When we got to Molly and Kylie's house, Mom went in to talk to their grandmother. Stephen, Ethan, and Ajax were playing catch on the sidewalk with some dumb ball from Molly's dumb-old wagon. Molly and Kylie and I sat on their front steps looking at the no-good, broken toys.

We opened up Molly's plastic purse. I counted the money she had gotten. I hate math, but I am good at counting money.

"How much?" Molly asked excitedly.

"Only one dollar and sixty-seven cents," I said.

"Oh," Molly sounded disappointed.

"That's pretty good," Kylie said. "Most of the toys we sold was all busted up."

"Please, Matthew," Molly begged. "We need more money."

I shook my head.

"Matthew, you got lots of money. Please, help us," Molly looked at me, with tears in her eyes. She goes and makes me feel all flusterdy again.

"All right," I spat out the words. "I'll give you enough to make two dollars."

"How much is that?" Kylie asked.

"Three pennies and three dimes," I said, "but you'll have to pay me back later."

"All right," Molly agreed. "Thanks." I looked away.

"When can we ask the Lion Man?" Kylie asked.

"Next time you come to my house." I swallowed hard. "But you have to ask him."

It was Molly's turn to swallow hard. She nodded her head.

Then Mom came out, "Time to get home!"

"Me too?" Kylie asked, holding up her arms for Mom.

"Oh, no," Mom said. "Inside, both of you. You don't get to come over when you go outside without permission."

Mom must have been upset. She didn't even hug the girls goodbye. Kylie was sure upset. She stuck out her tongue when Mom drove away.

During dinner, Ajax told Dad the whole story. He acted it out with his usual drama. He made his voice sound just like those boys—whining about how they were going to call the cops on Mom. Then he got Mom's voice just right—especially when she was talking about the cockroaches. Sometimes Ajax is alright. He could be a kid in movies. Like Mom and Dad would ever allow that. We're not even allowed to *watch* most movies.

"Those girls shouldn't be walking around alone," Dad said. "And why were they walking home from school so early?"

"They weren't walking home. They were walking away from home. Their mom got a job. They had a half day, and they were pulling a wagon," I said.

Dad looked confused. I don't know how he can interpret in two languages when he can't even understand me talking in just one language. Mom explained, "Missy got a new job. Since she will usually be working overnight, she can drop the girls off in the morning, grab some sleep, and pick them up after school. But, for the first few weeks of training, Missy has to work days—so a fourth grade neighbor walked Molly and Kylie home today after the school's early dismissal. The girls sneaked out while their grandma was upstairs putting MaKayla down for her nap."

"Do you know this neighbor who is walking them home from school?" Dad asked Mom.

"No," Mom shook her head with a frown.

"I know," Ajax said, puffing out his chest like a superhero. "I'll meet them after school and guard them home. And stand at their door like a soldier so they can't sneak away."

"You shouldn't be walking around town alone either," Mom said.

"If anyone bothers me, I'll punch them out!" Ajax jumped up from the table and began boxing.

"Sit down," Dad said. "I'm glad you want to protect the girls, but . . ."

Ethan interrupted. "We can form teams and walk them home together."

Stephen and I have to go help them tomorrow. Stephen calls it "damsels in distress duty." I call it *babysitting*.

CHAPTER 8

Backward and Forward

Ethan

THE NEXT DAY WAS a typical Friday for us Trellerts. Mom and us kids stayed home, finishing up the week's schoolwork, until it was time for Stephen and Matthew to escort the girls home from school. When Dad got home from his interpreting job, everyone gathered around the dinner table. Ajax, squirming in his chair, announced, "My Tuffies beat Ethan's Stuffies at football today, and my new toucan was voted MVP of the Tuffies. He's the greatest quarterback ever."

"Wow, you must have one tough team," Dad grinned, winking at me. He knows I usually let Ajax win. Ajax was even squirmier than usual tonight. Finally, Dad asked if he had ants in his pants.

"You wouldn't sit still either, if you were sitting on a tail of fire," Ajax announced.

"What do you mean?" Dad looked baffled.

"See?" Ajax jumped out of his chair, nearly spilling his bowl of chili. He whipped out a long and fuzzy red sock that was rather badly pinned to the seat of his pants. "I want to be called Comet, and I have a tail of fire."

Dad looked at Mom for an explanation. She laughed, "One night, Ajax went tearing out of bed to see the crowns on Stephen's head. I told him he streaked out of bed so fast that I might change his name to Comet. I explained that Ajax and Comet were both names of cleansing powders, but that comets were also things that dashed around the universe with tails of fire behind them. But, I was only kidding about changing your name, Ajax."

"Besides, son," Dad added, "at some point, you'll have to start using your real name, Aaron."

"I like Comet better," Ajax said.

"Well, Mr. Comet," Mom asked, "do you remember what your name means?"

"Nope," Ajax answered.

"Aaron means enlightened or illumined," Dad explained. "Remember last summer when I worked out West, and we explored that cave?"

Ajax nodded, "And Stephen and Ethan and Matthew went ahead with the only flashlight that still worked . . ."

I interrupted, "At Craters of the Moon, only it was Stephen who went ahead with the only flashlight. Matthew and I just followed so we wouldn't be in the tunnel in the dark."

Ajax went on, " . . . and Mom got stuck in the tiny tunnel, and I got sick . . ."

Mom dropped her muffin on her plate and groaned, "That just ruined my dinner."

Ajax was on a roll, ". . . so we had to leave Stephen and Ethan and Matthew in the cave, and Mom got scared and . . ."

Dad interrupted, "Before all of that, when all our flashlights were still working. When you turned on the flashlight, the area around you was enlightened or lit up. And God shines his light into our hearts. He shines his light in the world and the world can't put it out. Do you remember who Aaron is in the Bible?"

"Yep, he's the one who turned his stick into a snake," Ajax grinned.

"Well, God's the one who turned Aaron's staff into a serpent," Dad corrected.

"Then it ate the other snakes," Mathew added.

"Anyhow, back to your name, Aaron," Dad said.

"Yeah," Stephen interrupted, having stayed quiet as long as he could. "We named you Aaron because you're a mouthpiece, like Aaron was the mouthpiece of Moses. Guess that's why you never stop talking," Stephen teased.

"I do stop talking—when I sleep!" Ajax yelled. "You even talk in your sleep, Stephen."

"All right, guys," Mom tried to change the subject. "Ajax . . ."

"Comet," Ajax corrected.

"Comet," she went on, "do you remember what your middle name means?"

"Nope," Ajax muttered with his mouth full of Mandatory Salad.

"The baby name book we read said Gyasi was a name from Ghana, a country in Africa, the continent where your ancestors lived. Gyasi means 'wonderful child,' so it's a perfect name for you."

"A terrible name for him," mumbled Matthew.

"What?" Dad asked, glaring at Matthew.

"Nothing," Matthew said.

"Mom, you said you would tell me what Matthew's name means," said Ajax. Ajax never forgets his questions, even when they're days old.

"Matthew's name comes from a Hebrew word and means 'Gift of the Lord,' and he sure is a gift from God." Mom smiled at Matthew.

"Oh, I thought we named him Matthew because the book of Matthew says, 'Each day has enough trouble of its own,'" I laughed.

Stephen began, "I thought it was because Matthew was a tax collector who loved money . . ."

"That's enough," Dad said sharply. "Doesn't the book of Matthew warn that it's better to be drowned in the sea than to cause one of these little ones to stumble?"

"Please forgive me, Matthew," Stephen sighed.

"What's Matthew's middle name?" Ajax asked.

"Pedro," I answered. "It's Spanish."

"When we were in Colombia to adopt Matthew," Mom said, "everyone called him Pedro. It seemed like part of him, so we didn't want to take it away, but Stephen and Ethan had their hearts set on calling him Matthew. So, we named him Matthew Pedro."

"I hate the name Pedro," Matthew about snorted.

"All the people at your orphanage loved to sing your name," Mom said trying so hard to steer the conversation that she even attempted to sing. "So we decided to keep it. The English form is Peter. Do you know who Peter is in the Bible?" she asked Matthew.

"Duh," Matthew said. "He walked on water. Then he fell in."

"Peter means rock. And we've been praying for you to build your house on the rock, Jesus Christ," Dad explained.

"I want a house with a pool and air conditioning and a big yard. Not a rowhouse like ours," Matthew said.

"And we're praying that you build your life on Jesus and live in his perfect home forever," Dad said.

"What's Ethan's middle name?" Ajax piped up.

"Asher," I answered, "I'm Ethan Asher Trellert."

"I hate that name, Trellert," Matthew said. "Can't we change it?"

"Matthew, Trellert is an awesome name. It's a palindrome," Stephen said.

"What's that?" Matthew asked.

"A palindrome is a word that is spelled the same way backward as forward," Stephen explained.

"Huh?" Ajax asked.

"I'll show you," I said, getting up from the dining room table. I grabbed pencils and a piece of paper from a drawer in the kitchen, then stood beside Ajax. "Here." I ripped the paper in half and passed the other half to Stephen. "You show Matthew."

"Why can't Matthew sit down here with me?" Ajax complained.

"You know we can't have you and Matthew sit near each other," Mom began.

"Yeah, anyone who doesn't believe in spontaneous combustion hasn't been around when Matthew and Ajax sit by each other at dinner," Stephen joked.

Matthew jabbed Stephen with his elbow and glared at him. Stephen and I wrote out our last name and showed how it still made Trellert when you spelled it backward: t-r-e-l-l-e-r-T.

"Wow!" Ajax said.

"That's another palindrome," I said, and wrote it down backward and forward.

"Cool!" Ajax said. "Is that a palindrome?"

"No," I explained, writing the word *cool* both backward and forward.

"Do you want to see some more palindromes and read

some palindromic sentences?" I asked Ajax.

"Sure," Ajax cried, jumping out of his seat. "Are you coming, Matthew?"

"No way." Matthew said, plopping his elbows on the table.

The phone rang. Stephen ran to answer it, but it wasn't some girl calling for him. "Mom," he called, "Missy's on the phone. Molly had a fever at school today . . ."

"Oh, no," Mom exclaimed. Molly often has seizures when she gets a fever. Stephen handed Mom the phone. She nodded her head a few times, then said, "I'll be at the hospital in ten minutes." As she grabbed the car keys, she shouted to Dad, "Molly's fever was so high the doctors did a spinal tap on her. They're going to admit her, so Missy wants to stay with her at the hospital. Missy thinks it's too much for her mom to keep both Kylie and MaKayla. I'm going to run to the hospital then bring Kylie here."

CHAPTER 9

A Thirteen-Pencil Day

Lisa

EVEN THOUGH IT WAS late, Kylie bopped into the house. I drooped in behind her. "Joey!" Kylie shouted as she ran to him with her arms outstretched. "Guess what?" she said, her big brown eyes suddenly serious. "Molly's in the hopsital. She's sick."

"I know, Kylie," Joe said, patting Kylie's curls.

"I wish I could go to the hopsital. See my bear? Her name is Ole Katie, but sometimes I call her Poor Kitty-Kitty." Kylie held up a bedraggled bear that was covered with Band-Aids.

Joe kissed the bear, then asked, "And what happened to Ole Katie bear, who is sometimes called Poor Kitty-Kitty?"

"Oh," Kylie answered, "She got sick and had to go to the hopsital. The doctor put Band-Aids all over her. Will Molly come home with Band-Aids all over her?"

"I don't think so," Joe laughed and kissed Kylie's forehead. Joe greeted me with a kiss, "How is Molly?"

"The doctor gave her something to knock her out. She was asleep when I got there. The nurse said to come back tomorrow morning."

"I'm hungry!" Kylie said, "Let's eat!"

"Okay," Joe said, following Kylie as she skipped toward the kitchen.

"Thanks for cleaning up the kitchen." I looked around, grateful.

"I got to the schoolroom, too," Joe added, "Looked like you and Matthew had a tough time in there today."

"It was a thirteen-pencil day," I explained, referring to the number of pencils Matthew had dropped while working on his writing and math.

Joe asked, "Does he throw all those pencils?"

"No, his hands repel pencils, like opposite ends of a magnet," I sighed.

"Ajax asked if you could tuck him in. He said he had a question for you. And Matthew is just finishing up brushing his teeth. At least that's what he's supposed to be doing," Joe said.

"I'll check on him," I said, heading upstairs.

Matthew was pushing his toothbrush up and down in a sink full of water. "What are you doing?" I exclaimed.

Matthew, startled by my voice, jumped. His arms flailed wildly, splattering the mirror and walls with water. Then he slipped in the puddle that had formed at his feet. "See what you did to me!" Matthew shouted.

"Matthew," I attempted, "you're supposed to be brushing your teeth. What have you been doing?"

"I was pretending my toothbrush was the dry land, and the water in the sink was the seas. Did God make the seas and the dry land by pulling the water together to uncover the dry land, or by pushing the dry land up through water?" Matthew asked.

"You mean there really is a God?" Ajax yelled, popping out of his hiding place in the bathroom closet.

Matthew shrieked. I whirled around to face Ajax, who loved to scare Matthew just to hear his shriek. "Of course, there really is a God."

"Oh," Ajax said shaking his head, "I thought Bible stories couldn't be real 'cause they didn't happen anywhere." Stephen and Ethan exploded with laughter from their room next door.

"Ajax, get in bed," I ordered. "Matthew, empty the sink, dry the walls and floor, then brush your teeth."

"What about the seas and the dry land?" Matthew protested.

"Later," I barked.

"As for you, young man," I announced, marching Ajax into his room, "everything in the Bible is true and every historical event it describes happened in a real place. Tomorrow we'll look at a map. You will tell me every story you can remember from the Bible, and I'll show you where it happened."

"Ajax," Stephen shouted from his room, "are you real?"

"Duh, Stephen," Ajax yelled back.

"If there were no God, there would be nothing in the world. Really, there would be no world for there to be nothing in. If anything is, there must be a God," Stephen shouted.

"You're right, Stephen, but PLEASE, boys! Let me get Ajax and Matthew into bed." I stepped into Stephen and Ethan's room and signed, "Before they realize that Kylie is here, or I'll never get them to sleep."

"I want to go, too!" Matthew yelled, peeking in the door. He figured I was signing about something special that he didn't want to miss.

"Good!" I said, turning to face Matthew. Slowly and clearly I signed, "Go to bed." Matthew frowned and shuffled down the hall toward the stairs up to his bedroom. "Now, keep it down, guys," I reminded Stephen and Ethan, closing their door. Then I opened it again to say, "Go through your box of maps and find that big map of Bible lands, would you? We have some work to do with Ajax."

As soon as I stepped into Ajax's room, he said, "I know there's no God, 'cause remember when I hid from you, in the locker room?"

"How could I forget?" I asked, kneeling beside Ajax's bed and stroking his head. "When you ran away from me and hid in the men's locker room, where I can't go, inside a locker— where no one could see you!"

"Yeah, I know there is no God, 'cause when I was in that locker, I prayed for God to get me out. I said, 'God, if you don't get me out of here, I'll never see my mom and dad or Ethan or Stephen or even Matthew again.'"

"Well, you're not there anymore, are you? You didn't die in that locker room, did you?" I burst out, wondering if this day would ever end.

"But, God didn't get me out. Some man got me out."

"Ajax, God sent that man into the locker room. God caused that man to go down your row of lockers, out of all the rows in that huge room. And God helped that man see your little finger sticking out of that little hole in your locker. God did get you out of that locker. What did you want—an angel?"

"Yep!" Ajax exclaimed. "And before, when I tied myself

up with lots of ropes and told God to come down and get me loose? He never did. I had to get myself loose," Ajax spat out.

"When did you tie yourself up with ropes?" I asked.

"Remember when you taught Matthew about pulleys?"

"Of course, because after I taught him about pulleys, Matthew made a pulley, put Fluffernutter in a bucket and tried to lower him down from the balcony off Ethan and Stephen's room," I said.

"When Fluffernutter jumped out of the bucket and got on the neighbor's balcony, and you climbed over there to get him . . ." Ajax explained.

"Yes," I said, beginning to wish I hadn't asked the question.

"Then Matthew dropped the rope and the bucket down to the back yard, and ran to the third floor, 'cause he thought he was going to get in trouble."

"Yes," I gestured for him to get to the point.

"When you went to the third floor to tell Matthew not to put the dog in the bucket in the pulley again . . ."

"Not to put anything in any pulley, not to do anything at all, without asking his parents first, you mean?"

"Yeah, then I went to the back yard, and tied myself up with ropes and God didn't help me, but you said that God . . ."

"Wait a minute, Ajax. It's past bedtime. No more putting off bedtime with theological questions. We'll talk about this in the morning. Now, go to sleep."

"I guess you don't care if there isn't a God," Ajax said, turning away from me.

"Ajax, we'll talk about it tomorrow. Good night."

"Mom," Ajax yelled as I was closing his door. "You never told me Ethan's middle name."

"He told you at dinner. It's Asher."

I was feeling like Jesus when he cried out, "How long must I bear with this perverse generation?" Except without the prayer and with a whole lot of impatience. Okay, so I wasn't feeling like Jesus.

"What kind of name is Asher?" Ajax said.

"A Hebrew name, just like Ethan and Aaron. Good night," I yelled, closing the door.

"What's it mean?" Ajax shouted through the closed door.

"HAPPY," I exploded.

"Funny, you don't sound happy," Stephen commented from his room.

I groaned, then headed up to tuck Matthew into bed.

"Oh, Matthew," I said looking at a row of T-shirts he had decorated with fabric paint. "So this is what you've been doing all night. These shirts are beautiful." I picked up a little shirt with a painted triple-scoop ice cream cone topped with a bright red cherry. "Would you like to give this one to Molly? It's just her size. We could take it to her at the hospital tomorrow."

"Only if you buy it," Matthew said matter-of-factly.

"Matthew!" I exclaimed, "I bought all these shirts for you to decorate, and I bought all the fabric paints. And I've bought your decorated T-shirts to give to all your cousins for their birthdays. Don't you want to give one to Molly when she's sick?"

"This is my business, and it's for earning money. If I don't get enough money, how will I be able to live?" Matthew asked, nervously fingering a stack of little papers.

"Matthew, God has given you everything you need," I began.

"I need more money," Matthew said firmly.

I shook my head sadly. "If you don't want to give Molly a T-shirt, just forget it."

"Okay, I'll forget it," Matthew said with maddening cheerfulness.

"What are all those papers in your hand?" I asked.

"Coupons," Matthew said. "I have a big box of them. I cut them out of the newspaper every week, so I won't run out of money for food when I'm big."

"God promises to take care of his children. You can't trust in money—or coupons." I went on. "Do you know what expire means?" Matthew shook his head.

"Look." I took one of the coupons out of his hand and pointed to the expiration date. "It's from last year. This means it's no good anymore. Coupons expire and can't help you any longer, but God will always take care of you."

Matthew grabbed the coupon and clutched it in his fist with the others. "Look, Matthew," I tried again, but Matthew stared away and rocked absently. "All right, Matthew, we'll talk about this more tomorrow. Let me pray for you."

Back downstairs, Kylie was curled up on a sleeping bag on our bedroom floor. "You're sleeping in here?" I asked. She usually slept on the carpeted living room floor.

"I'm ascareda the dark, so Joey said he'd make me a nest on your floor and I could be a baby bird."

"I didn't know you were scared of anything," I said, tousling Kylie's curls.

"The dark is very scary. Especially at night," Kylie said.

Before dropping off to sleep, Kylie prayed, "Thank you, God, for fixin' Molly—okay, God?"

I added, "Thank you, God, for fixing Matthew, and Ajax, and me, and all of us—okay, God?"

CHAPTER 10

Best Bits

Ajax

THE NEXT MORNING, MOM went to the hospital to see Molly. Since it was Saturday, Dad, Kylie, and I made pancakes. First, we picked wild strawberries from our backyard. Then, Dad mixed up the batter, while Kylie and I chopped bananas. Kylie calls Dad's pancakes Bestest Bits because they are stuffed with bits of berries and bananas.

After breakfast, Dad shoved all the plates to one side of the table. Stephen and Ethan spread out a map. We took turns calling out stuff that happened in the Bible and finding the places where they happened. "The real places where these real events really took place," Dad kept saying.

When Mom came home she told us all about Molly. "Molly is awake, but is still holding her sheet and blanket tightly over her head, not speaking to anyone. I sat by her bed, stroking the fluffy spot that showed where Molly's hair was under her sheet. After I sang about six songs, her grip began to relax."

Matthew joked, "Funny your singing didn't make her grip tighter."

Mom didn't laugh. Or get mad. She just went on sadly, "Finally I could slip my hand under the sheet, just enough to stroke Molly's hair. I prayed for her, then she let me hold her hand, which was still over her head, holding the sheet. A minute later, the nurse came in to check on her. Molly pushed my hand away and her whole body became stiff."

"Like a soldier at attention?" I asked.

"Like a dead person?" Matthew asked.

"Like a treasure box, clamping shut the lid," Ethan said.

Mom went on, "I asked the nurse if she would talk with me in the hall. I got permission to bring one of you kids in to see Molly." Mom looked at Ethan as she went on. "I went back to Molly's room and told her I would be coming back to see her again soon and would bring a surprise with me."

I jumped out of my chair and ran upstairs. I burst back into the dining room with my stuffed toucan. "Mom," I began, "Molly really liked my toucan. Give it to her. That will make her quit hiding under the sheets."

"Ajax!" Mom gasped. "Are you sure you want to give away your toucan?"

"Yeah," I answered. "Last night, I kept thinking about God being real and about Molly. Then I got the idea to give her my toucan. When I woke up, I thought, 'If she's better, it's still my toucan. If she's still sick, it's her toucan. It's hers now.'" I handed the toucan to Mom, trying not to think about that empty spot on my Tuffies football team.

"Ajax," Mom said, "Would you like to come with me to give Molly your toucan?"

I tore out of the dining room again. "Where are you going?" Mom called after me.

"Gotta get my shoes!" I yelled back.

At the hospital, Mom and I took the elevator, then went through a bunch of halls until we got to Molly's room. A nurse was just leaving. "The doctor won't stand for her hiding under the sheets," the nurse warned. "He's due to show up soon, and he'll be in a hurry."

I stood by Molly's bed. "Molly," I whispered, making the toucan hop on Molly's covered head. "I came to see you. I'm Toco, the talking toucan." I went on talking in a squawky voice. Molly reached her hand outside the covers to feel the toucan's soft belly. She looked like a turtle coming out of its shell— except she poked out a hand, not a head.

I squawked and made the bird talk silly talk. Molly pulled the covers down, just enough to see the toucan's colored beak. I leaned down close to the toucan and grinned at Molly. "Here," I said, in my best bird voice, "I'm your toucan now."

Molly pushed the sheet away and held the toucan softly—as if it were real. When she looked at me, her eyes were shining. "Mine?"

"Yep," I said.

"Thanks," Molly whispered, as she hugged the toucan that used to be mine.

I kept making the toucan talk to Molly. Soon Molly giggled, then she laughed real loud. A few minutes later, we were laughing so loud that the nurse popped her head in the room. Molly stopped laughing right away, but didn't hide under the covers like a turtle. I made Toco talk to the nurse. The nurse said the doctor would want to meet the toucan too. "Okay," Toco the talking toucan squawked.

When the doctor entered the room, Mom stood up to leave. But the doctor told her to stay. "If that's okay?" He looked at Missy and she nodded. "And you two," he added, pointing to me and Toco, "are under doctor's orders to stay. Make your bird ask Molly how she feels," the doctor said, nodding at me. It seemed like Toco was an interpreter 'cause Molly talked to Toco, then the doctor talked to Toco, but it was me making it work. The doctor asked if Molly was ready to go home.

Molly said, "I want to take Toco home."

The doctor left the room saying something about papers. Then he turned around and said, "Molly has the flu. We'll give her medicine to keep the fever down, so she won't have more seizures. Nasty, late flu this spring. Even people who got flu shots have been getting it. If your family has spent much time with Molly over the past few days, you'll probably all get sick." Mom rolled her eyes. I couldn't believe she rolled her eyes at a doctor.

Later, I skipped down the hall toward the elevator. Mom looked at me so happy. She squeezed my hand and said, "What a great little man you are, Ajax. You helped Molly so much."

I said, "It's funny. I was so happy to get a stuffed animal for my football team. But, I was happier to give it to Molly. I feel like popping."

"That's because you went for the best bits," Mom answered.

"Like Dad's pancakes?" I asked.

Mom explained, "You could have kept your toucan and been happy. But you loved Molly, gave up your toucan, and now you're way happier."

But that afternoon I wasn't so happy sitting in the living room all alone. Mom poked her head in. "There's nothing to do," I complained.

"Oh, you and Ethan were planning to play stuffed animal football," Mom said.

I nodded sadly. "But I don't have a full team, so Ethan's playing chess with Stephen. Dad is taking Kylie home and said I couldn't go with him. What can I do?"

"Ajax, do you want to call Molly and see how she is?" Mom asked. I ran into the kitchen to pick up the phone. It made me happy again to hear how happy Molly was. And I saw that Mom was cooking my favorite dinner—ravioli.

When I hung up, Dad walked through the front door with Kylie. "No one answered the door, so I brought Kylie back," he said.

"That's funny," Mom said. Ajax just hung up with Molly. "I guess her grandma is watching her and didn't hear you knock on the door."

"I brought another surprise," Dad said pulling a bag from behind his back.

I bounded over to him. "For me?" I yelled, ripping open the bag.

"Wow! Thanks, Dad!" I ran back into the kitchen. "Look, Mom!" I shouted, holding up a stuffed football player with a football in his hand.

"There's more," Dad said, bending down and pulling the football out of the player's hand. The football and the football player's hand had strips of that shoe strap stuff that sticks, so the ball could stick in the player's hand. "You can really use this football for your Stuffies versus Tuffies games," Dad explained.

"Thanks, Dad," I yelled. "And, thanks, Mom."

"I didn't do anything," Mom laughed.

"You took me to see Molly," I shouted.

"Thank you, Ajax," Dad said, "for being such a man to little Molly. You knew just what she needed and you ran to give it to her. I'm proud to have such a fine young man for my son."

Enough mushy stuff. I ran off shouting for Ethan, "Now my Tuffies can beat your Stuffies any time."

At dinner that night, I told all about my visit to the hospital. Matthew asked, "Didn't you see any dead people? I can't wait to see dead people. I bet they look funny."

Kylie smacked Matthew in the stomach, and Mom and Dad

didn't even yell at her. Probably they wanted to hit him, too, for saying something so mean. Maybe Matthew even felt bad, 'cause he didn't blow up. I just went on, telling them all about Toco the talking toucan.

"Do you know what 'toco' means in Spanish, Ajax?" Ethan asked. "It comes from a word that can mean 'to touch.' 'Toco' means 'I touch.'"

"I guess you sure touched Molly's scared little heart today, Ajax," Mom said. "Giving away your toucan was a very loving thing to do."

"No one ever tells me I'm loving," Matthew shouted. He pushed away from the table, knocking over his chair and spilling his glass of water. Matthew ran out of the room, still yelling.

Dad went out to where Matthew was crying in the living room. I wanted to see what happened next, so I followed Dad. Dad put his hand on Matthew's shoulder, but Matthew pushed him away and glared. "I hate you all. No one ever tells me I'm loving."

I said, "It's funny that Matthew hates us because we don't say he's loving." But no one was paying attention to me now.

"Matthew," Dad began, "do you want to be a loving person?"

"Yes," Matthew sobbed.

That was a surprise, but all Dad said was, "That's good. God has so much power that he can change you from someone who is afraid to love into someone who loves to love. Let's ask him to change you."

CHAPTER 11

Milk and Miracles

Joe

IT HADN'T BEEN ONE of our better mornings. Nikki had invited us to her church, where she was singing in a children's choir for the closing service of the missions festival. Lisa and I were rummaging through closets looking for dress shoes. Then I was in charge of breakfast for Ajax and Matthew, while Lisa searched for Ajax's tie and tried to find out if Missy would either pick up Kylie or gather dress clothes for her.

I poured milk into Ajax and Matthew's cereal bowls and slipped outside to grab the Sunday paper. I'm sure I wasn't even gone a minute. I heard the shouting before I even got back in the house. I ran for the kitchen, where I found milk dripping down the walls, off the cupboards, and from the ceiling—not to mention, all over Matthew and Ajax.

It took me fifteen minutes to sort it all out. Matthew wanted a little more milk in his cereal. He asked Ajax to pass the milk. Ajax did—a bit too roughly. Some milk sloshed onto the table. Offended, Matthew shoved the milk jug—hard and fast—back at Ajax, splashing milk on his pajamas. Angry, Ajax hurled the jug at Matthew. By the time I got there, there was no milk in the container, but there was milk everywhere else.

I was in the middle of my little counseling session with Ajax when he burst out, "I want to move to Africa. I don't belong in this family. I want to live with my birth mother."

"We're going to a missions festival," I responded. "Maybe, when you're big, you can be a missionary in some African country. Your mom and I would love to visit you there. But, you're dead wrong about not belonging here with us. God planned for you to be here—in this family—before he even made the world. And your birth mother wouldn't let you throw milk on your brother, either. Now, what did you do that was wrong?"

Finally, the boys, subdued by now, were dressed for worship at Nikki's church. Almost dressed, that is. Lisa was wrestling with Ajax's tie.

"Why can't I wear my jeans and T-shirt?" Ajax moaned. "I wish I lived with my birth mother," he added.

"Oh, believe me, your birth mother would make you dress up for church," Lisa said, as she wrenched his tie this way and that.

"I wish I lived in Africa," Ajax said. I took over adjusting Ajax's tie and his attitude, while Lisa tried to tame Kylie's curls. "I don't have to get all dressed up when we go to our Deaf church," Ajax argued. "How come I have to get all dressed up when we go to a Black church?"

"Because," I explained, "you need to be all things to all people. That means you sign when you go to the Deaf church where you can wear your jeans and tennis shoes. At Nikki's church, you can listen in English, and you get to wear your best clothes."

By ten o'clock, we were spruced and spiffed to a shine, but there was still no word from Kylie's mom. We stopped at Kylie's, but Missy didn't answer the door. "Probably sleeping after that long night at the hospital," Lisa said as she rummaged through the glove compartment looking for paper and pencil. Finally, Lisa dropped the hurriedly scrawled note through the mail slot, and we took off with Kylie, who was wearing the dirty, rumpled clothes she had on when she arrived Friday night.

While I drove to the church, Lisa drilled Matthew and Ajax on their manners. "Remember, you have to answer everyone who speaks to you with 'Yes, ma'am,' and, 'Yes, sir.' And, if someone serves you something during the meal, say, 'Thank you.'"

"What if I don't like it?" Ajax whined.

"Ajax," Lisa retorted, "it doesn't matter if they give you Swamp Water Yuck Balls, you say, 'Thank you.' Understood?"

I fixed the rear view mirror on Ajax in time to see him nod solemnly. A few minutes later, we filed into the building—the boys in their best shirts and ties, and Kylie in her old blue jeans and Mickey Mouse T-shirt.

As usual, the singing was rousing enough to hold the boys' attention. Nikki shone in the children's choir. The guest preacher was from Uganda, and his message was entitled "Joy to the World."

"It's nowhere near Christmas," Matthew had protested despite Lisa's efforts to shush him. The sermon began with creation—God creating the animals, then Adam. God shaping Eve from Adam's rib; God creating the male and female and pronouncing them good. The preacher went on to Adam and Eve's sin, prompting the need for missions. As I was practicing my interpreting skill of predicting where a message was heading—Babel and the scattering of the nations, Abraham being blessed in order to be a blessing to the nations—the pastor explained that God slew an animal to make the clothing to cover Adam and Eve.

Matthew jumped to his feet and yelled, "That's awful!" In one stunned second when my body couldn't move, my brain ran wild. This is not the way you want your child to behave when you visit a church. Finally, my limbs unfroze. I grabbed Matthew's hand and ushered him out the side door for his second counseling session of the day.

Outside, Matthew sobbed, "Why would God kill an animal? Animals are way better than people."

I explained that God made people for his glory. Matthew countered that God made animals for his glory, too. "And people are made from dirt," Matthew added.

"No," I paused, "Adam was made from dirt. Eve was made from Adam's rib."

"Yeah," Matthew rolled his eyes, "Men are from dirt."

"Well," I recovered enough to say, "God made people, but not animals, in his image."

"Why did God make boys and girls anyhow?" Matthew asked, still crying.

"For his glory, and for moms and dads to love," I put my arm around Matthew. He didn't push it away.

"Why did God make moms and dads?" Matthew asked.

"For his glory, and so children have big people to love them and take care of them."

"But why? Matthew shouted. "Why moms and dads, and boys and girls? Not just girls?"

I looked down, as if I would find the answer on the sidewalk and noticed that my fists were clenched. "For his glory."

"But I hate being a . . ." Matthew began.

I cut him off, wondering how much the people inside could overhear. "Listen, Matthew, I know you're not comfortable in the body God gave you. But God the Son didn't have a body. He had never gotten sick or been tired, hungry, thirsty, or tempted to sin. He could be everywhere at once."

"Like Six Flags and Disney World at the same time?" Matthew was beginning to be interested.

I ignored the question, "Do you think it was fun for him to become a person—a baby?"

Matthew shook his head, "And a boy."

I went on, "A boy who wet himself and couldn't even get his own dinner—a boy with a body just like yours?"

Matthew gasped, "I thought he was God."

"Perfect God and perfect man," I explained.

"But my body doesn't fit right," Matthew said hopelessly.

I prayed—one of those quick and desperate lassos heavenward, hoping to capture some wisdom—"Let me draw him with your cords of love."

"Matthew," I began, still not sure what to say. Then God's wisdom and my words began to flow. "Your body may feel strange to you, but Jesus was God. His body really was totally foreign to him. Do you know why God became a man with a body like yours?"

"To die for my sins?" Matthew said.

"Yes, to die the death you deserve for disobeying God and not being thankful for the way he made you. And to perfectly love, obey, and glorify God in his body—as a baby, a boy, and a man." I looked at Matthew. For once, he didn't look away. "Do you believe in Jesus?"

Matthew nodded and looked down.

I crooked his chin with my hand, "I don't mean do you believe that he lived. Everyone knows that. Do you love him and trust him?"

"Way more than I trust you," Matthew said.

I ignored that. "Do you know he's the best there is—better

than Six Flags and Disney World?"

Matthew said, "Yeah, but I still want to go to Six Flags."

I persisted, "But if you had to choose between Jesus and Six Flags, which would you pick?"

Matthew was quiet a long time. Finally he said, "I'd pick Jesus."

I nodded. "Where does Jesus live?"

Matthew pointed upward, toward heaven, I guess. I took his index finger and pointed it toward Matthew's heart. "The Bible says everyone who believes in Jesus is joined with him."

Matthew frowned, "I don't feel joined with Jesus."

I continued, "Sometimes you don't feel like I love you, but I do. So it doesn't matter if you feel joined with Jesus. The Bible says everyone who believes in him is joined with him and has died to the old sin and risen to live in new ways. That means what you can't do, Jesus in you can do. Do you understand that?"

Matthew brightened, "You mean Jesus can do the math I can't do?"

I laughed, "No, even Jesus had to work to learn things. But Jesus in you can help you work hard without getting mad, giving up, or throwing pencils. And Jesus was content in his body. Jesus came to glorify God in his body, and Jesus lives in you to glorify God in your body. Do you understand?"

"Mostly," Matthew nodded.

I added, "You're dead to wanting your own way more than wanting God's way."

"And alive to wanting God's way?" Matthew asked.

"Yep. The Bible says you have been crucified with Christ and it is no longer you who live but Christ who lives in you. And the life you live in the body—in this body that God has given you," I pulled Matthew in for a hug, "you live by faith. Jesus in you can trust and obey God in this body until God gives you a new body."

"I'm going to get a new body?" Matthew asked excitedly.

"Yes, when Jesus comes back, you'll get a perfect body that you'll live joyfully in forever. Now, how 'bout we slip back inside before everyone gathers in the dining room to feed their imperfect bodies?"

We walked back into the service during the closing prayer.

Thankfully, everyone had their heads bowed—except Kylie, who grinned and waved at us. I put my finger to my lips, hoping she wouldn't break out into her usual exuberant greeting.

Soon, we were sitting at a table with Nikki's family in the fellowship hall. The pastor stood to welcome everyone to the international dinner. "Let's bow in prayer," he continued.

"Deaf people don't bow their heads when they pray," Matthew whispered—far too loudly.

"This isn't a Deaf church, so bow your head," Lisa hissed back, staring at Matthew until he obeyed.

Finally it was time for our table to go through the serving line. Beside each dish was a card giving the name of the dish and the continent it represented. As Lisa read the names of the African foods—ground nut stew, callaloo, doro wat, and fufu—Ajax announced, "I don't think I'll move to Africa after all. I don't like the food."

Lisa's eyes grew wide, and her face flushed. Damon began to chuckle, followed by Nikki, Stephen, and Ethan. A number of people near us in the food line began to laugh. Finally, Lisa and I joined in.

As we sat all the children back at the table, I sighed with relief. Now I could enjoy my fried chicken and greens, and talk sports with Damon. Just at that quiet moment, Ajax piped up, "Mom, I'm sure glad they didn't give us Swamp Water Yuck Balls, like you said they would."

Lisa's face reddened, but Damon snickered, "I don't like Swamp Water Yuck Balls either."

CHAPTER 12

A Crack in the Concrete

Matthew

AFTER THAT HORRIBLE DINNER at church—except the fried yams were good—we stopped at Molly's house to see how she was feeling. We weren't allowed to come inside with Mom and Dad. "You might get sick," Mom said. As if we'd want to go in their junky old house.

Stephen and Ethan sat on the front stoop playing Rock, Paper, Scissors. Ajax was jumping from the top step down to the sidewalk. I stood on the sidewalk, tearing up coupons and watching them blow away in the wind.

"Back in the car, boys!" Dad shouted. "Time to head home!"

But I still had a few more coupons to tear up. "Matthew, you're littering," Mom began.

I scowled at her, "You said God didn't stop, like coupons do. That he would always take care of me. He didn't take care of me when I was a baby. No one did!"

I looked away angrily. Mom doesn't think I know anything. But I heard the social worker tell her about my papers. The ones that said N.N. for No Name. The ones that said I never had any visitors all the time I was a baby in the hospital.

Mom was quiet. Then she pointed to a little bird hopping on the sidewalk. "Matthew," she began, "the Bible promises that not one sparrow falls to the ground without God knowing it, and he says you're worth more than many sparrows."

I was looking away from Mom—at a crack in the sidewalk. I bent down and picked up a little flower that poked out through a crack in the sidewalk. The little flower had five white petals with lines of pink. "It's a star flower," I said.

Mom knelt beside me and said, "It's beautiful. I can't imagine how it blossomed here, in a crack in the concrete. Sometimes, God gives flowers a garden home. Sometimes God provides someone to weed the garden and water the plants. And, sometimes, God causes a flower to blossom through a crack in the cement. But it's always God who makes the flowers grow. And the flowers glorify God, by doing what he made them to do."

"Like me? Sometimes?" I asked.

"Like you," Mom smiled. "God helped you grow through a crack in the sidewalk when you were alone so long in the hospital, then brought you to a loving orphanage, then to your garden home with us." We got into the van together.

Back at home, Mom and I made quesadillas for lunch. Ethan didn't feel like eating. He went to the living room and went to sleep. Right on the floor—the best dance floor in the whole house, where I wanted to practice dancing all afternoon. I had to dance around him. Later, Stephen lay down beside Ethan. He asked me to turn down the music. Now I had to dance over both of them.

I asked Mom to come see my dance. Ethan yelled at me. I just tripped over him, and he yelled at me. Instead of yelling at Ethan, Mom put her hand on his forehead. Then she asked Dad to run to the store to get some juice. No fair! Ethan yells at me, and Mom sends Dad out to buy juice for him.

Dad and Ajax went to the store. "I don't feel so great myself," Dad said when he came home. "I think I'll grab a pillow and some blankets and join them."

Dad went upstairs, and Ajax sort of crumpled on the floor. No one yelled at him when he fell on the floor.

"Ajax, what's wrong?" Mom asked.

"I'm expensive," Ajax said.

"Yeah, right," I said. "You're worth about a dollar."

Mom glared at me. She's always telling me not to glare at people, but she glared at me.

"I mean, I'm exuberant," Ajax moaned.

I know that word because people always tell Ajax he's exuberant. But he didn't look very exuberant.

"I mean, I'm exhausted," Ajax cried, putting his head in

his hands.

"Oh no," Mom groaned. "Are you sick, too?"

Dad came down with two pillows, and he and Ajax cuddled up on the floor. That did it. That ruined my dance floor. I stomped up to my bedroom.

Later, Mom tried to make it up to me. She came up to my room to see my dance, which I was practicing in my bedroom. In my little bedroom, instead of in the big living room with lots of room for dancing.

I didn't even show Mom all of my new dance. I sat down, right in the middle of the dance. "I can feel where it's missing," I told Mom.

She said my dance looked wonderful, but I wasn't talking about the dance. "I feel it missing, where God took it out."

Mom looked at me confused. She does that a lot.

"Like he said in church this morning. Where God took out Adam's rib to make Eve. I feel it missing inside me. That's why it's better to be a girl. 'Cause nothing's missing inside girls."

Mom said, "No, Matthew. God made Adam to give life by giving up his rib. God made Eve to receive life by receiving Adam's rib. God made men to give life by giving up their lives. God made Eve to receive life within her."

She put her hand on my head to pray for me. "Oh no," she exclaimed. "Not you, too." That was the first I noticed that my head was hot like fire.

The next day, Mom was the only one who wasn't sick, so she walked Kylie home from school. By Tuesday, Kylie was sick and stayed home with Molly. No one had to walk the girls home all week. That was the good part of being sick—no walking babies home from school.

It was a sick, quiet week at our house. Just Mom reading us books and us sleeping on the living room floor.

Sunday afternoon, Ajax popped up like a Jack-in-the-box. I hate those Jack-in-the-boxes. The scary way they pop out. He said it felt like Easter.

Maybe having a fever fried his brain. We already had Easter. Back in March, we acted out Ajax's favorite book *Haffertee's First Easter*. I wore the Haffertee Hamster costume, and Ajax wore the Howl Owl costume. He ran around the house flapping those huge wings and saying, "Tu-whit, to-whoo," a thousand times. We made a tomb out of clay and rolled away a big stone. We met at a park so early it was still dark outside, and we shone our car lights so we could see everyone signing until the sun came up.

Dad popped out after Ajax and said, "It feels like Easter because it's like we're rising from the dead." Ethan, Stephen, and I came into the dining room, too. It seemed like ages since we had eaten real food, and Mom had a feast on the table.

The next afternoon, Ajax and I were in the kitchen. We were drawing pictures for a contest. The adoptive families' group was having a contest for kids who are adopted. "Kids who *were* adopted," Dad always says. I don't see what difference it makes how you say it. Dad says his working with words buys my food and markers and the stuff I use to make costumes for my plays and dances. He said, "You *were* adopted. That was done in the past. You *are* my son. That goes on forever."

So the contest is for kids who *were* adopted. We are supposed to draw what our family means to us. If we win, we get money. Ajax drew a picture of our whole family. He used the people-colored markers to get everyone's skin color right.

"Ajax, your picture is so happy. I wish we could keep it instead of sending it to the contest," Mom said.

"I'll make another one for you, Mom," Ajax said, grabbing another piece of paper.

Ajax decided to title his picture, "My family means I belong."

"You sure do," Mom said. "You belong here with us."

I crumpled up another piece of paper and threw it on the floor.

"Matthew," Mom said, "you're such a great artist. What's the trouble this afternoon?"

"I don't know what to draw," I said.

"That's funny," Mom said. "Our walls are plastered with your drawings. Our basement is full of murals you painted as backdrops for your performances. You're the most creative person I know. I didn't think you ever ran out of ideas." Then she asked, "What does your family mean to you?"

"Nothing," I said.

Mom made a funny, sucking sound. "Oh, that's the problem," Mom said. "You can't draw a picture of what your family means to you if it doesn't mean anything. Why don't you just skip the contest? Draw something you'd like to draw."

"But, I want the prize money."

"Then I guess you're stuck, unless your family starts to mean something to you," Mom said.

The phone rang. It was Molly. Mom said, "I'm so glad you called. Are you going to school tomorrow? Should I send the boys to pick you up?"

There was a long pause.

"Hold on, a minute," Mom said, looking at the white board on our kitchen door. It was a tangle of colors—blue for kids' stuff like baseball and soccer games, and my performances— even though we don't go out for those, I make Mom put them on the white board 'cause they're way more important than soccer games. Red's for Mom's stuff, and green means Dad's stuff.

Stephen opened the kitchen door and bumped into Mom. He asked why she was standing in the doorway.

"Molly is asking when she can come over. I'm looking for some free time."

"Probably won't find it in the kitchen. Try Aisle 3. I can't believe Molly asked for something."

"I can't believe you noticed," Mom said as Stephen ran out the back door, kicking the soccer ball to Ethan. Picking up the phone, Mom said, "How 'bout coming for dinner Friday night for Ajax's birthday?"

Molly must have asked to talk to me because Mom handed me the phone. "Ajax's birthday is Friday," Molly yelped. "We gotta get the lions soon."

"Okay, tomorrow," I said and hung up the phone. I told Mom, "I want to put on a play tonight." Dad and I had built a stage in my bedroom. It made my bedroom crowded, but it even had curtains that opened and closed. "Can everyone watch my play tonight?" I asked.

Mom checked the calendar again and told me everyone but Stephen could see my show, since Stephen would be at his fencing class. "That's okay," I shrugged, "Stephen can see it Saturday, since I'm planning two performances anyhow."

That gave me an idea. I grabbed the papers and markers and ran up to my bedroom.

I came to dinner carrying my picture. I was on a large stage wearing a sparkly black and red costume. There were lights shining, and a spotlight shone right on me. "This is for the contest," I announced.

Mom said, "Wow! How colorful!" She frowned, "What does this show about what having a family means to you?"

I pointed to the bottom of the page where I had drawn the backs of five heads in the audience. "That's you guys," I said.

"Oh," Mom was quiet for a minute. Then she grabbed a pencil. "Let's fill out the entry form."

I wrote my name and address. "What's this?" I asked, pointing to the next line.

"You need a title for your picture," Mom explained.

"A family gives me an audience, and that makes me a star."

After dinner, I said, "Tickets for my play only cost a dollar. Refreshments will be fifty cents."

Dad announced that there would be no performance if the tickets cost money, so I gave everyone tickets. "Your *free* tickets," I said.

When they came up to my room to see my show, Ajax sat in the wrong chair. "Sit in that chair," I told him, pointing. "That one is Mom's chair." I told Ethan to be my helper. "Turn off the light," I said. "Open the curtains. Now, start the music. Now turn the light back on." Ajax began clapping. "Don't clap yet," I told him. I began to dance, and everyone clapped. I love putting on shows.

After the show, I went downstairs to put away the leftover refreshments. The *free* refreshments.

Even from the kitchen, I could hear Ajax. He was in bed— sort of. At least he was hopping in and out of bed. "Mom, I have a bunch of questions tonight. They're popping in my head."

"Just like you're popping in your bed," Mom laughed.

"What decides when your baby teeth come out?" Ajax asked. He rattled on, "What's the difference between a rod and a staff? And if potatoes are roots, why do they grow roots when you put them in water?" Little kids don't know anything.

Mom said, "Which question do you want answered first?"

"All of them!" Ajax shouted. I bet the neighbors could hear him.

The front door slammed. That meant Dad was home from

picking up Stephen at fencing class. Stephen went pounding up the stairs. He didn't even ask about my play.

"I'll write all those great questions down, and we can look for some books next time we go to the library," Mom said.

"Internet, Mom," Stephen yelled as he ran into his room. "Gotta start sometime."

CHAPTER 13

Plunge Right In

Ajax

MATTHEW AND MOM WERE in Matthew's room on the third floor doing schoolwork. I wasn't allowed in even though they were reading about a carved boat that goes in lakes and rivers and goes all the way to the ocean. I wasn't allowed in because Matthew says he can't think when I breathe. And I don't just breathe when Mom reads books—I run and kick a ball and shoot hoops and still understand the story.

I took my LEGO boat into the bathroom to do my own school. I wondered if I could flush my boat down the toilet and run outside fast enough to see it swoosh by under the bars of the drain on our street. My experiment wasn't working out very well. My boat disappeared and I ran fast outside, but didn't see anything under the bars of that drain. Not even water. So I got a flashlight and tried my Fisher-Price boat. I flushed the boat down and ran as fast as I could, but I still couldn't see anything in the drain. Not even with a flashlight. I went to my toy box to look for another boat. When I came back to the bathroom, there was a river on the bathroom floor.

I'd seen Dad fix the toilet. So I went to the closet and got out the plunger. I plunged hard and flushed again. Now there was sort of a lake in the bathroom. I figured I better fix this before Mom came downstairs and got upset. I took the top off the toilet. I was pulling out the pieces when Stephen walked into the bathroom and yelled at me. I ran after Stephen with the plunger. Ethan took one look at us and ran to the third-floor stairs yelling, "Mom, you better get downstairs. Quick! Ajax took the toilet apart, and when Stephen yelled at him, Ajax got mad and attacked him with the plunger, and now . . ."

Mom flew down the stairs. She threw all our towels on the bathroom floor, which was sort of a mess now. She made me take off my clothes, which were sort of wet. Then she made me go to the kitchen, in my underpants—since our only bathroom was messed up—to wash my hands and practically my whole self. Then she ordered, "Upstairs for dry clothes, then march back to the kitchen!" I was in for it.

"What were you doing?" Mom asked.

"School," I answered. I told her all about the science experiment and how I couldn't see the boat through the drain on the street. "You always tell us to keep on trying, so I tried again," I explained, "but I broke the toilet, so I tried to fix it so you wouldn't be upset."

Mom sighed and put her head in her hands. I didn't know if she was thinking of how to punish me or praying for patience. I hoped she was praying. Finally she said, "So, you broke the toilet, and you were trying to be a man for your mom and fix it."

I nodded, then looked down at the floor, waiting for my punishment.

"I'm proud of my little man," she said.

"For breaking the toilet and messing up the bathroom?" I couldn't believe it.

"You should have asked before doing science experiments. But, then you were trying to help—you saw what needed to be done and tried to do it. Dad only has a morning interpreting job today. He should be home by lunchtime, and you two men can work on it together." She looked at her watch, "Oh boy! I can't believe it's time for lunch already."

"Don't worry, Mom," I shouted. "I'll help you get lunch out."

"Thanks, little man," she smiled, "but you better clear things up with Stephen first. Don't we have a rule against attacking people with plungers?"

I ran upstairs and pounced on Stephen, who was reading in his bed. By the time Mom came to check on us, Stephen and I were wrestling on the bed. "Did Ajax ask you to forgive him, Stephen?" Mom asked.

"One hundred percent," Stephen laughed. "Even if it was

90 percent bounce and 10 percent words."

During lunch, Stephen explained that the drain on the street is a storm drain for rainwater to go down so our street won't flood during big storms. He said my boats never went there. He drew a map on his napkin. His map started at our toilet and went underground, then all the way to the water treatment plant where he said toilet water is cleaned. I couldn't understand how a plant could clean that water, but Ethan explained that plant is another word for factory—except they don't make toilet water, they clean it.

Stephen started to tell how they clean the water, but Mom said no more toilet talk at the table. So Stephen shut up, but he used the other side of his napkin to draw the way they clean the water. And Mom said this is why we need cloth napkins—so Stephen couldn't draw pictures of sewage treatment plants during lunch. Then Stephen said what I needed was to go down a manhole. I asked what that was, but Mom said, if I ever went down a manhole, Stephen would have to go in to get me out of the manhole, so Stephen shut up again.

We were just finishing lunch when Dad walked through the front door. I yelled, "You can't use the bathroom because of my boats, and Stephen's not mad at me now about the plunger, and—you and me—we're gonna fix it now because Mom says we better fix it before someone needs it."

By the time Dad and I got the bathroom clean and working, it was nearly time to go get the girls at school. After all of us being sick for so long, no one could remember whose turn it was to get them. Matthew said, "Stephen and I will go." We were all shocked. Mom felt his forehead to see if he was still sick.

So Ethan and I got to play stuffie football. My team creamed Ethan's. Dad came up from his basement office to see how my new quarterback was doing. Stephen and Matthew stomped through the front door.

"Everything okay?" Mom called from the kitchen.

"Yeah," Stephen answered, then pounded up the stairs. Dad went back to his office in the basement. Ethan and I played another game. This one was a battle, but I came out on top in the end. Then Mom called us all for dinner.

Ethan and I ran into the dining room. Stephen stumbled

down the stairs with a book in his hands. Dad came up from the basement and said, "Wow! Tablecloth and candles and flowers on the table!" He asked mom what she had squeezed out of her day to pull off this fancy dinner.

"Only one of the kids," Stephen joked.

Mom looked around. "Where *is* Matthew?" Ethan ran up to the third floor to get Matthew but came down alone.

"How 'bout the backyard?" Dad said. But, in our yard, it didn't take much looking to see he wasn't there.

"All this time, I thought he was up on the third floor doing his art projects, or his dance, or . . ." Mom looked worried.

"Has anyone seen him?" Dad asked.

"He did come home with you, didn't he, Stephen?" Mom asked, sounding panicked.

"Yeah." Then Stephen added, "I think so."

"This is no time for the absent-minded professor bit, Stephen. Did he come home with you or not?" Dad growled.

"Yes, he came home with me, but he didn't go upstairs when I did. He went down to the basement."

"Are you sure?" Dad said, running to check his office. But there aren't any hiding places there. "I never even heard him come down," Dad said. Now it was his turn to sound worried. "Okay, let's pray," Dad said, taking Mom's hand. "Then, Mom and Ajax, you search the house. Ethan, Stephen, and I will comb the neighborhood. If we don't find him in fifteen minutes . . . Well, let's pray."

CHAPTER 14

Molly Speaks

Molly

KYLIE AND MATTHEW AND me hid the lions under the back porch. We hopped up the porch stairs. We bumped into Joe at the door. Lisa ran to us, and she was cryin'. "Are you all right?" she yelled, grabbing all three of us. We couldn't breathe—all bunched up in her hug. "Where were you? What were you doing? And why are your hands and feet covered with mud?"

"Don't cry," Kylie said, wiping Lisa's tears with her muddy hands. "We got a present for . . ."

I slammed my hand over Kylie's big mouth, making Kylie's face more muddy. "Yuck," Kylie spit right on the porch. "You got mud in my mouth, Molly."

"Don't tell nothin' more. It's a surprise." I was so happy. Was—'til I saw Lisa start to look mad.

Ajax and Ethan and Stephen came to the door too. We were all lumped in the doorway. "Why don't you two," Joe pointed to Ethan and Stephen, "take Ajax upstairs and play a little overtime in the Stuffies-Tuffies game?" Joe began.

"Aww, I always gotta miss the good stuff," Ajax moaned.

"Lisa, take the kids in the living room to wait for me," Joe said. I'll call Missy to let her know the girls are all right."

Uh-oh. I should have known Joe would call Mama. We forgot to plan out how Kylie and me would get home. We forgot to plan out how we wouldn't get in trouble.

When Joe hung up the phone, Lisa asked, "Was she worried?"

"She didn't even know they were gone."

"Well, I didn't know Matthew was gone either," Lisa said.

Now she looked sad, instead of mad.

"I told her we'd bring the girls home as soon as we figured out what happened. Now," Joe said lining us up, like we was gonna play a game, 'cept Lisa and Joe didn't look like fun. "Where have you been? Matthew, I thought you and Stephen walked the girls home from school."

"We did," Matthew said. "And Stephen and I walked home. Then I walked back to their house. It's her fault," Matthew said pointing at me. "She said we had to go because of Ajax's birthday on Friday."

Joe raised his eyebrows and looked at me. I never been in trouble at Joe and Lisa's before. Kylie and Ajax—they been in trouble plenty 'a times. But not me. I gulped.

"And hers," Matthew poked Kylie. Kylie batted his finger away. "She said the Lion Man might eat little girls, and, if he ate them, I'd feel sorry I didn't go with them."

Joe yelled, "What lion man?"

Lisa yelled, "Where did you go?"

"Well, Molly wanted to go to the Lion Man's," Matthew began.

"You went to someone's house—someone you didn't even know?" Lisa said, looking madder and madder.

"It's Ajax's fault," Kylie explained. "Because he liked the lions. And Molly's. 'Cause she wanted to get them."

"For Ajax's birthday," I added.

"But we didn't know how much the Lion Man would sell 'em for, and we ain't allowed to sell MaKayla to get enough money." Kylie went on, "So, we sold our toys in a wagon."

"So, today, after Stephen and I got home, I took Dad's phone," Matthew began.

"You took my cell phone?" Joe asked, slapping his hands to feel his pockets.

"Yeah, from your office. Here it is," Matthew pulled the phone out of his jacket pocket. "It's no good anyhow. I tried to call 911, but your phone doesn't work."

Joe turned on the phone. "You have to turn it on, Matthew. I had it off when I was out interpreting and must have forgotten to turn it back on." He put the phone in his pocket. "Wait! Why did you want to call the police?"

Matthew explained, "When the Lion Man opened the door,

he looked mean and mad—like you look now. I told Molly she had to do the talking, but she just stood there, looking at the ground. Then I thought maybe we should call the police. Just in case."

"I was so scared," I said.

"So," Kylie bopped up and down while she spoke, "I said, 'Excuse me, Mr. Lion Man Sir, I hope you don't eat kids, and how much for the lions 'cause we only gots two dollars?'"

Now I could tell that Lisa was just trying to look mad, but her eyes were smiling. "And what did Mr. Lion Man Sir say to that?" Lisa asked.

"He said, 'How much what for what lions?'" Kylie answered making her voice boom like the old man's.

"Then," Matthew interrupted, "the Lion Man said, 'So, it's "Please, Mr. Lion Man, sir," when you want something from me, huh? Aren't you the sassy little thing who stuck out her tongue at me not long ago?'" Matthew glared at Kylie. "It's stupid to stick out your tongue at a Lion Man. Especially if you want something from him."

Joe's eyebrows shot up, and he asked Kylie, "How do you know this man?"

Kylie bounced up and down. "That day Lisa taked us home from the park. That's the day Ajax said he liked the lions, and Molly said we got to get 'em for Ajax, and I said that man probably eats kids, and . . ."

"Kylie, you shouldn't stick your tongue out at people," Joe said. Then he yelled, "And you shouldn't ever go to someone's house when you don't know them."

Lisa turned to Matthew and asked, "Then what happened?"

"Then Molly pointed to the lions, like this." Matthew put his head down and sticked both arms straight down.

"Then the man said, 'Oh, how much for those lions?'" Kylie said in a growly voice.

"And," I said, "Kylie told him 'bout Ajax and his birthday, and he gived us the lions for nothin', but we didn't know how to carry them here, and the man laughed and said they were plastic, so I carried one, and Matthew carried one and we hided them under the porch, and don't tell Ajax."

Then Kylie popped onto Joe's lap and said, "And please let us stay for dinner."

"Not this time," Joe said like he was still real mad. Kylie jumped off his lap and stamped her foot. "Only when you ask your mom or your grandmother first, and we come get you." Joe explained.

Kylie clenched her fists and rubbed her tears so the mud spread all over her face. Joe put one arm around me and one arm around Matthew, 'cept Matthew wiggled away. "Now," Joe began, "what you kids did today was foolish and dangerous." I looked at the floor.

Joe went on, "Something awful could have happened to you. Don't ever, ever, ever, go anywhere without asking first. Do you understand?"

We nodded, even Kylie. "And, Matthew, don't ever take anything that belongs to someone else without asking. Understand?"

Matthew nodded his head without looking up.

Finally, Joe's face looked softer. "And, Matthew, even though you were very wrong not to ask us first, I'm proud of you for one thing." Matthew looked surprised. "You were a real man, to protect the girls and try to take care of them." Joe smiled at Matthew and gave him a thumbs up. "So, while you're accepting your punishment . . ." Matthew groaned, but Joe went right on talking. "You can remember that Mom and I are glad you tried to protect the girls."

Kylie grinned. "So now we can stay for dinner?"

"No, little one, you always have to ask your mom before you go anywhere." Kylie shook her hair, which looked as wild as her face, and wailed. "No matter how much you cry, Kylie, I'm taking you home," Joe said. "But, first you three must tell me you'll never again leave home without asking first. And, never, never, never go to a stranger's house. Do you understand?"

Matthew and I nodded our heads. "Kylie?" Joe asked. Kylie was still cryin' but her head bobbed up and down. Joe folded us into his arms and prayed, thanking God for keeping us safe. Then he drove us home. "Good-bye, Molly," he said hugging me. "Both of you, remember: "Don't ever, ever, ever, go anywhere without asking first." I said okay. Kylie just ran into the house and slammed the door.

CHAPTER 15

Even Matthew Had the Sense

Joe

After I took the girls home, Lisa met me in the dining room. The candles were cold stubs and dinner was even colder. I wondered why Lisa hadn't started eating dinner with the kids.

"I think we should take the lions back and make Matthew apologize," Lisa said.

"He gave them to the kids," I protested.

"What else could he do?" Lisa countered. "The kids shouldn't go around asking for handouts."

"So, what am I supposed to say? 'Hello, Mr. Lion Man Sir, I'm Joe Trellert, and this is my son, Matthew. I'm here to return what my son and his friends finagled from you this afternoon.' How can I make Matthew apologize? We keep telling him to love people, and that's what he was doing. Or trying to do. And we keep trying to get Molly to ask for things, and that's what she was doing."

"I just don't think we can set a precedent of letting our kids walk up to strangers and ask for their things," Lisa objected.

"I hardly think we have to worry about precedent. It's not as if there's going to be another set of lions looking inviting on someone's porch."

"How about I take them back to him?" Lisa said, reaching for the car keys. "I'm the one who thinks they should be returned, and I'd actually love to meet him. You must be starving. You eat, and Matthew and I will be right back."

"You don't really think I'm going to let you do that," I sighed. "I'll do it." I grabbed the car keys and shook my head, "Even Matthew had the sense not to send a girl to the Lion

Man's alone."

Famished by now, I watched Matthew crawl under the porch to get the lions. We got in the car with the lions, and I gave Matthew the wet rag Lisa had handed me. As I followed Matthew's directions to the Lion Man's house, he washed mud off the lions.

"You sure this is the right house?" I asked Matthew. I didn't want to give my spiel to the wrong person.

Matthew nodded. "Yep. I remember it had paint peeling on the porch floor, and the window had blue curtains with ducks on them. The man was wearing a red shirt with a hole by the pocket, and he had one gold tooth. There were two big pots of plants, and there they are," Matthew pointed. Sure enough, there were the blue curtains in the window and, seeing the wrong side of the curtains, I could just barely make out the silhouettes of birds flying.

Matthew and I just stood on the porch, while I tried to figure out how to begin. The front door opened and the Lion Man—what else am I supposed to call him?—said gruffly, "Well?"

"I'm Joe Trellert, and I think you've already met my son, Matthew. I guess these are yours," I said pointing to the lions we had set on the porch.

"Not any more," the old man chuckled.

"Well, I didn't want the children to be rude . . ." I faltered, unsure of what to say next.

"First visitors I've had for years," the man said. "And the only ones I ever want to see again."

"Well," I began awkwardly, wondering if the man was telling me to leave. "They're too young to go gallivanting about alone. And they can't just go asking people for . . ."

"Bah! They'll learn manners soon enough. Then they'll ignore me like everyone else. Let them have the lions."

"Well, thank you," I said, wondering if Lisa would be satisfied with this turn of events. The man closed the door. Matthew and I trudged back to the van—with the lions.

Back at home, Lisa looked at me expectantly. I signed, "We'll talk after dinner." But, because dinner was so late, the usual bedtime flurry followed immediately afterward. It was late when I finally told Lisa everything I had learned about the

Lion Man.

"What's his name?" Lisa asked.

"Don't know," I sighed.

"Does he live alone?"

"Didn't ask," I answered.

"Poor guy," Lisa mused. "He's just a sad, lonely man." Then she brightened, "I have an idea!"

I groaned, which is exactly what I tell the boys not to do when Lisa announces an idea. She went on, oblivious, "Friday is Ajax's birthday. What if I wrap up the lions, pack a picnic dinner, and we have a little birthday party right on the Lion Man's porch?"

She was smiling broadly now. "I could even bring a few balloons. Maybe Stephen would make a banner on the computer. We could decorate his porch."

I laughed, "If you'll forget the banner and balloons, and leave it at dinner and a birthday cake, I'm in. Or, maybe, just birthday cake. After all, we don't even know if the Lion Man has any teeth."

"He does," Matthew, who had evidently been hiding in the hallway, popped into the dining room. "Remember, I told you that one of his teeth is gold?"

I shook my head at him, preparing to lecture him about eavesdropping. But Lisa was in a brainstorming blizzard, "Okay, just fried chicken and potato salad. And maybe some fresh vegetables and fruit. I already invited the girls for dinner Friday night. I'll wrap the lions and let the man see Ajax open them. Ajax will be so excited. Oh, but, what if Ajax notices the lions are missing from the front porch?"

I just shrugged and marched Matthew upstairs.

So, Friday night, we picked up Molly and Kylie and drove to the Lion Man's. Ajax, Kylie, and even Molly prattled, but everyone else was quiet—nervous. "I got somethin' for you, Ajax, and I ain't gonna tell you what," Molly repeated in a singsong voice. "You bringed 'em, didn't you, Lisa?"

Lisa nodded. I looked at her and whispered, "Don't worry," I said. "If he does eat kids, I'll call 911." I pulled my cell phone out of my pocket and grinned. I parked the van at Farquhar Park. The older boys grabbed the baskets of food. I took the two now-wrapped packages out of the van. Lisa said, "Okay, kids, just a short walk down this block. Dad and I will knock on the door. When he comes out, you say, 'Surprise!' Then I'll invite him to Ajax's birthday party."

"Wait," Ajax said. "I'm having a party? I thought we were going out for dinner."

"We are—sort of," I smiled at him.

"What am I supposed to call this man?" Stephen asked.

"What man?" asked Ajax.

Lisa and I answered in unison, "Sir."

The Lion Man had a name after all: Gus. Kylie mispronounced his name as Guts, much to his delight. "Sir Guts, the Lion Man," he said with a roar. When Ajax opened his gifts, he gasped and Molly lit up. Ajax picked up both lions and kissed them. "Twin lions!" he exclaimed with delight.

Before long, Kylie was curled up in Gus's lap. They ate as a team, Kylie taking a few bites from a piece of chicken, then passing it to Gus while she started on a fresh piece. Molly sat beside them, her eyes shining. Ajax sat between his lions, pretending to feed them, and chattering about what he would name them. Matthew was unusually quiet and calm. Ethan had Gus's cat in his lap.

Lisa asked Gus if he had grown up here in York. "My family moved here from Bamberg, South Carolina, in the late '20s. My pap heard there were jobs up North, even for us Black folk."

"Like me?" Ajax asked.

"Yep, Black like you, 'cept you're a mite young to work. These days, at least," Gus went on. "My pap found a job this side of the Mason-Dixon line."

"Lion?" Ajax asked.

"No, line. The line dividing Pennsylvania from Maryland and West Virginia. They first made that line because one King Charles gave Maryland to one man, and another King Charles gave this area to another man . . ."

"William Penn," Stephen said.

"Yep, and the two families fought over the land and took it to court. Mason and Dixon were the men who marked out the boundary with stones. Then, during slave times, it was the line between slave states and free states. Anyhow, my pap got on a train. We young 'uns cried the day he left."

"I don't remember when my dad left," said Molly. Gus

pulled her onto his other knee and then continued. "A year later, Pap sent word we should come. Mama and us young 'uns got on a train with a basket of food and a satchel of clothes. Rode up through Baltimore."

"That's where the aquarium is," Ajax interjected, looking up from his lions.

"With the sharks!" Matthew shrieked.

"Well, there was no aquarium back then," Gus laughed. "Then we crossed the Mason-Dixon line. Past that little station in New Freedom, past farms in Glen Rock, through the Howard Tunnel."

"Where the rail trail is being built!" Ethan exclaimed. "We can't wait till it's finished," he added.

"Yeah," Stephen said, "now, when Mom gets the biking bug every October, we have to drive to Maryland, bike to the Pennsylvania border, ride back to where we started, then drive back to York. Life will be easier when the Pennsylvania side of the rail trail is open."

"Well," Gus went on, "it used to be for trains, not bikes. Coming through that Howard Tunnel into the bright sunlight and all the hope we thought was stored for us up North was like . . ."

"Entering Narnia?" Stephen asked.

"Well," Gus hesitated, "maybe like Narnia before Aslan was on the move." He went on, "Speaking of Narnia, I made a little something for my kids. Maybe you'd like to see it?" He lifted the girls gently off his lap and motioned for us to follow him inside.

It had gotten dark on the porch. Gus's living room was darker still, but he flicked on the light and pointed to a wall that was lined with deep shelves. Stephen whistled. Matthew gasped. The four boys moved toward the wall. Molly tugged on my shirt. "Up, please?" she asked. Kylie scampered to Ethan, clambered into his arms, and pointed with delight.

It was hard to know where to look first, but Gus pointed to the table on the far side of the room. Ajax yelped, "Look! It's Narnia!" Ajax ran to the elaborate set-up. There was the castle of Cair Paravel overlooking a beautiful sea. "And look, there's the Stone Table, and the lion, Aslan—dead." Ajax's voice trailed off.

"Just push this button," Gus said, pointing to a knob near Ajax's hand. Ajax pushed it, and Molly yelped when the lion leaped off the table and jumped to the ground.

"Wow!" Matthew said.

"How'd you do that?" Ajax asked.

"Electricity," Gus answered. "If I put you on a table and pumped enough of it into you, you'd fly up in the air too," Gus chuckled.

"Don't get any ideas," Lisa said to him. "Gus, this is amazing."

"Used to show all this at the fairgrounds," Gus began. "Years ago."

Stephen was looking at a chess set. "Carved it myself, I did," Gus said.

"That's a Middle Earth set, isn't it?" said Stephen, pointing to dwarves lined up as pawns. Gus nodded and smiled, pleased to have someone appreciate his handiwork.

Molly pointed to a diorama of a little girl beside a huge Christmas tree. Gus showed her another button, and, when she pushed it, the tree sparkled with lights and spun slowly around. Molly's eyes grew wide. "Bet you don't even know that's from *The Nutcracker*," Matthew said contemptuously. But Molly clapped her hands with delight.

"And look, over there," Kylie pointed to a circus scene, where a clown was perched on the end of a high diving board with both hands clasped over his eyes. Kylie didn't wait for permission. She reached down from her roost in Ethan's arms and popped the button with her fist. She let out a gusty laugh when the clown stepped forward and fell off the board. Then she giggled when a tiny parachute opened and brought the clown fluttering down to the bathtub below him. Her giggles turned into a big yawn that ended with hiccups.

"Oh, Gus, we need to get the girls to bed. But, this was such fun." Lisa hugged Gus and asked if they could come by again soon. Kylie, urging Ethan toward Gus as if she were riding a horse, fell into Gus's arms and tried to kiss him. Instead, she hiccuped in his face, which set her giggling again. "G'night, Guts," she finally managed, between giggles and hiccups. "Sir Guts, the Lion Man, who used to be scary."

Molly wriggled out of my arms and skipped over to Gus.

She tugged at his sleeve until Gus put Kylie down and smiled at her. Molly looked down at the floor. "Thanks," Molly whispered.

Gus scooped her up in his arms. She looked small and frail next to his towering frame. "What's that? I couldn't hear you. Be careful! I eat little girls who mumble."

Molly bit her lip, but Gus was grinning. Molly smiled, a little at first, then widely. Molly shook her head, then laughed, "Careful, I eat big Lion Mans who tease me." Gus rubbed his nose against Molly's, then handed her back to me.

Ajax threw his arms around Gus's legs and said, "Thanks for my lions. I decided to name one Rex and the other Wrecks."

"Sounds like a bunch of double talk, my man." Gus said, thumping Ajax on the back.

"They sound the same, but they're different words. One is my name from my birth mother. It means king, like a lion is the king of the jungle."

"And like Aslan is King of Narnia," Ethan said.

"Like the Lion of Judah is King of kings," Stephen added.

"But I don't spell it like my birth mother did. I hate silent letters," Ajax continued.

"I think, you just hate silence," Stephen teased.

We headed out the door. "Happy Birthday, Ajax!" Gus called out, as we scrambled into the car.

"Grrrrr!" Ajax roared.

CHAPTER 16

The Lighthouse

Lisa

THE REST OF THAT weekend hurried by. Sunday night, Ajax was watching Joe as he packed a suitcase. "How come you have to leave?" Ajax asked glumly.

"I'm interpreting a conference out of town," Joe answered.

"You won't be able to see my baseball game Tuesday," Ajax pouted.

Joe patted him on the back, "I know. I wish I could be there, but I'll call you that night to hear all about it."

Stephen walked into the room, "Phone's for you, Dad."

Ajax ran off to play soccer with Stephen. A few minutes later, Joe found me in Matthew's room, reading a book to him. "My out-of-town assignment was just canceled," Joe said.

I brightened. "What happened?"

"Only one Deaf person had signed up, and she just let the conference coordinator know that she was canceling. She has the flu. So, they don't need an interpreter."

Then Joe started signing, "I have an idea!"

"Tell me, too," Matthew yelled, trying to grab Joe's hands.

"Let me talk it over with Mom to see if it will work," Joe told Matthew. "Besides, it's time for you to go to bed. Maybe you'll have a surprise in the morning."

"I hate surprises," Matthew said as he tumbled into bed.

After tucking all the boys into bed, Joe and I began planning a trip to the ocean the next day. "Maybe we could stay overnight?" I mused.

Joe said, "Well, I'm not sure Missy would want the girls to miss two days of school."

"You want to bring Molly and Kylie, too?" I exclaimed as I rushed to the phone. Missy hesitated, however, worried about getting in trouble with the school.

"I'll have Joe write the note for the school. He can sign it Dr. Trellert. That should impress them."

"I didn't know he was Dr. Trellert," Missy said.

"Well, his degree is in linguistics, but he can call it a marine biology field trip. We'll look at crabs and clams, study shells, look at all the shellfish in a tidal pool, identify gulls and sandpipers, and . . . Hang on a sec, Missy." I covered the mouthpiece and said, "Joe, isn't there a wildlife refuge we can go to?"

He nodded, "And a lighthouse not far from the wildlife refuge."

I turned back to the phone. "Missy, we'll go to a wildlife refuge and see all kinds of birds. We'll see a lighthouse—if we can, we'll take the girls up to look around. Ajax can fly his kite, so I'll teach them about the wind, and we'll study tides and clouds. Oh, Missy, they'll learn so much in one day at the ocean that the school will owe them a day off when they get home." So, it was decided that we would pick up the girls at seven-thirty the next morning.

At five-thirty, a full hour before the alarm was set to go off, Matthew pounded on our bedroom door. I bolted up in bed and shouted, "What's wrong?"

Matthew burst through the door and said, "So, what's the surprise?"

"We're going to the ocean," I crowed. "Molly and Kylie are coming too."

Matthew glared at Joe, "You mean, you're not earning any money today?" Matthew stalked out of the room and shut the door noisily behind him.

Joe groaned, "It's like living with Scrooge."

"Well, don't you be a Scrooge," I laughed.

"At least Scrooge lived alone," Joe went on.

"Matthew lives alone, too. The rest of us are hardly even furniture in his little world. Don't let him ruin this day," I said.

Joe strode to the door and called Matthew. I held my breath to see what was coming. When Matthew came into our room, Joe said, "Matthew, I know you worry about money. Even though today almost everything we're doing is free, I know you're worried that I'm not out earning money today. If you want to earn money today, I can call Mrs. Graham. I saw her washing windows the other day, and she could probably use some help with her spring cleaning. Since you're so concerned about our family having enough money, the money she gives you for helping her could go right into the family budget, so you won't have to worry about my work being canceled today. How 'bout it, would you like to work for Mrs. Graham today?"

I held my breath. Matthew looked at Joe angrily. "You don't want me to come, do you?"

"Not if you're going to worry about money or ruin things for everybody else. If you'll trust God to take care of our family and live happily under my authority, then I want you to come. But, you'll have to decide. Let me know when you've made up your mind."

The other kids and I got breakfast and started scrambling around the house, packing up food, books, sports equipment, blankets, sweatshirts, and beach toys. Soon everyone was in the van, except Matthew and Joe.

"I want my kite," Ajax yelled.

"It's in the laundry basket," I answered, "With the bedspread, sunscreen, sweatshirts, buckets, and shovels. The binoculars and bird books are in the backpack, and there's a cooler of food. Anything else anybody needs?"

"Only Matthew," Ajax said quietly. Just then, Matthew came bounding down the front stairs, with Joe right behind him. "Here he comes. Hurray!" Ajax yelled.

We picked up Molly and Kylie and began the long drive to the beach. I read books to the younger children all morning, interrupted frequently by their cries of, "Are we there yet?" Stephen wondered aloud about the sanity of having six kids spend seven hours in the car for only four or five hours at the ocean.

"Actually, by the time you figure in the drive from the beach to the wildlife refuge, the drive around the wildlife refuge, and the drive to the lighthouse, it's well over eight hours in the car," Joe corrected.

Stephen groaned and went back to his book.

"What's the ocean like?" Molly asked.

"Like the sky, only moving-er," Ajax answered.

Kylie kicked Stephen's book out of his hand. "The ocean is like God," Stephen said, "Awesome and other, yet restful and peaceful."

"Huh?" Molly asked.

"He means that the ocean roars like a lion, and tickles your toes like a kitten," Ethan explained, tickling Molly's toes where they stuck out of her sandals. "You'll see soon enough. See that bridge up ahead? That will take us across the bay."

Molly and Kylie gasped at their first sight of the bay. Excitedly, the children pointed out gulls, herons, and sailboats. A few minutes later, Joe parked the car a block from the beach. All the children tumbled out. There was a shuffle while the day's supplies were distributed among the older children. Then we began our short-but-long trek to the beach—with the older boys, weighed down by buckets and baskets, helping the girls straggle down the block. As soon as they hit the sand, Stephen and Ethan dropped their armloads of stuff. "Far enough that we won't have to move back when the tide comes in," they said, which set up the first science lesson of the day.

Stephen and Ethan kicked off their sandals and ran toward the waves. Matthew and Ajax chased after them. "Can I go, too?" Molly pleaded, jumping up and down and grabbing Joe's hand.

Joe took Molly down to the water's edge. "You comin'?" Molly asked Kylie.

"No way," Kylie said, shaking her head. Her hair, arranged in puffball pony tails, bobbed vigorously. "This is the goodest sandbox I ever saw."

"I'll stay with Kylie," I laughed.

Stephen, Ethan, and Matthew swam out from shore, then rode the waves back. Joe stood between Molly and Ajax, holding their hands. Every once in a while, Molly turned and waved to me, her face shining. A big wave came, and Molly and Ajax tumbled down. But both children were smiling when they popped out of the water again.

"Look," Kylie yelled, pointing to a hole she was digging. A few nearby sunbathers noticed Kylie and laughed with delight.

Stephen, Ethan, and Matthew came hurrying back to the blanket, asking for sweatshirts through chattering teeth.

"Matthew, come help me dig a hole," Kylie ordered happily. Matthew hesitated. "C'mon, Matthew," Kylie added, smiling at him. Matthew grabbed a shovel. Soon, Matthew had dug a deep hole. Perched on the edge of the hole, Kylie shouted encouragement: "That's good, Matthew. Keep digging."

Ajax ran up the beach and threw himself on the blanket, shivering. He wrapped himself in his towel. "I don't see how Molly can stay in there," Ajax mumbled through his cocoon. "It's so cold!"

"Sorry, Molly, I'm freezing," Joe said, holding her hand as he led her back to our beach blanket.

With blue lips, Molly jumped up and down. "Please take me swimming, Ethan," she begged. Ethan took off his sweatshirt, grabbed Molly's hand, and ran with her back to the waves.

"I'm hungry," Matthew announced. He dropped his shovel and sat beside me while I arranged lunch. Kylie was lying on the sand, her face and arms hidden in the hole. She was scraping more sand out with her hands. Every few seconds, she tossed a spray of sand upward. Most of it fell right back in the hole, only to be sprayed upward a moment later. Kylie inched forward—pushing with her toes and straining to reach deeper into the hole. Suddenly, she fell in. Her little legs fluttered where they stuck out from the hole. Peals of laughter skipped along the beach, as Kylie pushed with her arms and wriggled out. Her face popped up, freckled with sand but grinning. "I falled in," Kylie announced. "But I ain't hurt, and my hole's deeper and deeper."

Ethan came back with Molly. "C'mon, Joe. Will you take me swimming?" she pleaded.

"I'm still freezing!" Joe protested.

"I'll take her, Dad," Stephen said, taking Molly's hand.

"Then Molly needs to warm up and eat lunch," I shouted after them.

"I ain't cold," Molly shouted back, her whole body shivering.

So the delightful day went on, with Kylie wriggling in and out of her sandy hole and Molly accompanied by a constant round robin of swimming buddies. I watched as Ajax and Joe held Molly's hands. Ajax loved pulling her up after she got knocked down by the waves. "You don't have to worry about

Molly," Ajax yelled back at me, "I'm her lifeguard."

After my short and freezing turn in the water, I took the kids for a walk, and the girls gathered a bucket of shells to take home. I pointed out all the insects, plants, and birds. When the tide went out, the children found crabs in the tidal pool. Joe suggested a sand sculpture contest. Stephen made a chess board, then sculpted the chess pieces. He fashioned sand castles for the rooks, sea horses for knights, and a Neptune figure for the king. Matthew, Ajax, and Molly stayed out of the water long enough to make a whale.

"What's that?" Matthew asked pointing to Ethan's sculpture.

"It's a rockhopper penguin," Ethan began. "They live in southern Chile and . . ."

"Cool!" Matthew interrupted. "A penguin with a Mohawk!"

After Joe helped Ajax fly his kite, we reluctantly began gathering up scattered clothes and toys. We tramped back to the van and headed for the wildlife refuge. Kylie fell asleep. Ajax and Molly loved using the binoculars, although I'm not sure they ever aimed them at any birds. We moseyed along Wildlife Drive—spotting a green heron shimmering in the late afternoon sun, spotted sandpipers scurrying along the shore, and ospreys swinging up from the water triumphant with fish.

Then we headed to the lighthouse. All the kids, except for Kylie who was still sleeping, got out of the van. Spotting someone who looked official, Joe approached him to find out whether the lighthouse was open. Judging from the children's crestfallen faces, I guessed it wasn't.

Then the children applauded and the man unlocked the door and accompanied Joe and the children inside. From the upper windows, the children waved to me. When I waved back, Kylie stirred. She opened her eyes and looked around. "Where is everyone?" she asked. I pointed up. Kylie gasped, "They might fall down and break their heads," she whispered in awe.

I explained that the children were safe behind the window. I told Kylie about lighthouses. "This one is just for decoration, but other lighthouses still shine out at night to warn ships about the nearby sandbars and rocks. The light keeps sailors safe, even during dark storms."

"That's what I need in my room," Kylie said. "So I won't be

ascareda the dark."

"God is there with you, Kylie, even in the dark. Especially in the dark," I assured her.

"But if I had a lighthouse, I could 'member God was watchin' me, like the lighthouse watchin' over the boats," Kylie said.

"Lisa, did you see me?" Molly yelled with sparkling eyes as the group returned to the van.

I hugged Molly. "I sure did. And you sure had a happy day."

"The bestest day," Molly said.

We drove to a restaurant. The waitress who seated us at a table asked, "These kids all yours?"

"No," Joe laughed, "But I bet you can't guess which ones are."

CHAPTER 17

Light in the Dark

Nikki

MAY RIPENED TOWARD JUNE. All over the city, children were itching for summer. Especially me. Summer is my time to write and illustrate books and hang out at the Trellerts—since they live across the street from me, and since I can go there to get away from my pesky twin brother and sister.

On Memorial Day, Matthew and I turned his backyard into an art park. We organized stations with crates filled with art supplies. Other kids from the neighborhood showed up, eager to join in the fun.

Stephen and his friend Ryan were painting a huge mural on the poster boards Matthew had taped to the fence. The mural spanned the universe, starting with paintings of the other galaxies, moving to our solar system, then zeroing in on a huge globe of the earth. The globe then zoomed in on a map of North America, then the United States, then Pennsylvania. Eventually the painting focused on York. The final scene showed the boys themselves, working on a mural of the universe. Ethan and his friend John Allen were painting a parade of animals around the border of the mural. Not just everyday camels, lions, and bears. This mural had aardvarks, sea otters, horned lizards, and pangolins.

"What a fantastic mural!" Miss Lisa exclaimed, coming out of the kitchen with a pitcher of lemonade.

"Oh, we're not done yet," Stephen answered.

"Not nearly," Ethan said.

Along the back porch wall, Matthew had set up the lattice boards that were supposed to be covering the crawl space under the house but had been broken since last summer. Pembrook, and Janalia—I call them PB and J—even though Pembrook was my grandfather's last name, I don't know what my mom was thinking naming her baby boy and girl such obvious PB and J names. She must have been hungry for peanut butter and jelly sandwiches after that long labor with twins. And it's very funny that we moved across the street from a family with a dog named Fluffernutter. Anyhow, PB and J and Ajax were weaving ribbons through the lattices. The colorful patchwork included strips of a baby blanket that had unraveled, and curlicues of foil.

At the sculpture table, Matthew had dumped all the boxes, wrapping paper tubes, paper towel tubes, old plastic containers, and other odds and ends he had scoured the house to find. "We need that piñata stuff," Matthew said. "Please," he added.

"I don't have any tissue paper," Miss Lisa apologized.

"Not tissue paper. The gooey stuff with newspapers," Matthew explained.

"He means papier-mâché," I said, looking up from the boxes I was gathering for my sculpture.

"Yeah, so we can paste our sculptures together, then paint them," Matthew added.

So Miss Lisa went back to the kitchen. A few minutes later, she came out with a roasting pan filled with wheat paste and a big stack of newspapers. Matthew used a shoebox for the base of his sculpture. Then he taped a cardboard tube in place and covered it with wheat paste. Then he taped another cardboard tube on and papier-mâchéd it. He had to hold it a long time until it set. I've never seen him be still for so long. One by one, the tubes went up or out. Just when it looked like he was done, he grabbed another shoebox. He made a second sculpture, the same way, but different angles.

Stephen glanced over at Matthew's sculptures and yelled, "Compliments on your complements!"

"What do you mean?" Matthew asked, snarling a bit.

"If you put the sculptures together, they would fit beautifully. Not quite like pieces of a jigsaw puzzle . . . still they complement each other. Stephen came over to Matthew's sculptures and outlined their edges. "So, I said, 'Compliments,' meaning praise, 'on your complements.' Just don't ask me to spell either word."

"They don't add up to 90 degrees," I said. For someone who is so smart in math, Stephen could be sort of dumb.

"A complement can also be something that completes something else. The complement of a mathematical set completes the universal set." I should have known better than to argue with Stephen about math.

Stephen walked back to the mural where he was painting parts of an atom in the lower right-hand corner—the only spot on the mural that was not yet covered. "There," he said with satisfaction: "Panorama: From Pluto to Protons."

"By way of Pennsylvania," Ethan added.

Mr. Joe opened the back door and walked out on the porch. Miss Lisa blurted out, "Oh, is it dinner time already?"

"That's a nice greeting. Maybe you need a manners role-play," Mr. Joe said. I had heard about the manners role-play. Matthew told me that Mr. Joe played my step-dad washing our car. "I got home early and thought I'd check out the fun."

Miss Lisa relaxed, "Well, in that case, I'm glad to see you.

"Come out with us," I shouted. Five minutes later, Mr. Joe had changed out of his suit. He began working at the sculpture table.

I told him I was making a princess puppet. "I think I'll call her Princess Nikkisha. That's my real name. I have a fancy name, Nikkisha. And I have an everyday name, Nikki. Sort of like reversible cloth," I added, looking at a two-sided strip of fabric. "And I'm lucky too, 'cause I get to be every kind of kid there is."

"What does that mean?" Mr. Joe asked. He was taping an upside down butter container on top of an oatmeal box.

I answered, "I'm the oldest one of my mom's kids." Mr. Joe nodded, smiling at PB and J, who he thinks are adorable. "But, in my dad's family, I'm the baby. My dad lives in New York and the rest of his kids are older than me. But, in my step-dad's family, I'm the middle child, 'cause he has two kids that are older than me and two kids that are younger. So, I get to be all the kinds of kids there are: oldest, youngest and middle."

Ajax, who was walking over to the sculpture table to see what we were doing, snorted—he actually snorted—"You don't get to be a boy."

"You mean, she doesn't have to be a boy," Matthew said.

"No, I mean she doesn't get to," Ajax insisted. "Boys are great, huh, Pembrook?"

Pembrook nodded, but Matthew rolled his eyes. "I hate being a boy."

Mr. Joe looked at Matthew, who was looking at his sculptures. He said, "Matthew, look at the sculptures you made. You did such a great job on them. See how they go together perfectly?" He went on, "That's how God made men and women. He made them to fit together. Making both men and women was God's idea. Something he did for his glory. And it glorifies God when you live as the man he designed you to be."

Enough of that. I ran off to get more fabric for my princess. When I came back to the sculpture table, Matthew was still staring at his sculptures. Looking right at Matthew and squinting a bit, I could see those pasty white sculptures reflected in Matthew's dark eyes—looking a bit swimmy.

Now it was Matthew's turn to run to the fabric table. He grabbed black yarn and all the ribbon. He asked Miss Lisa to bring him paper plates. "The hard kind," he added.

Miss Lisa seemed to know what that meant because, sure enough, she came back with the kind of paper plates you want for summer picnics of baked beans and potato salad—not the cheap kind that soak your lap before you know it.

Matthew taped the plates to the top of his sculptures, so they looked like faces. He slathered wheat paste to glue the faces to the necks. He cut hundreds of pieces of black yarn and stuck the yarn on top of one face. "Hair?" I asked.

Matthew didn't even answer, but I could tell by the way he was styling it that I was right. Finally, he cut another hundred pieces of ribbon. Red, black, pink, gold, purple, silver, green, orange, blue like the sky in summer, and blue like the sky at night. He curled each ribbon by whisking it over the scissors. Then he arranged the ribbons on the other sculpture.

"Yep," he said. It took me a while to realize that he was finally answering my question. The ribbons made the girl's hair look a bit like Miss Lisa's, which—to tell the truth—was getting a bit wild in the breeze and humidity.

Looking at the crazy curly hair on Matthew's sculpture reminded me that I hadn't finished my own project. I got back to work on my puppet, but kept glancing at Matthew. By the time I had finished my puppet, Matthew had papier-mâchéd a paintbrush into the boy sculpture, where its hand would be. He was cutting a piece of cardboard. It looked like a big, softly-curved Pac-Man until he cut a hole in it. "A palette!" I exclaimed.

"No," Matthew answered, "It's that wooden plate an artist uses for paint."

"That's what I said," I muttered. There's no point arguing with Matthew about words. I thought he'd put the palette in the boy's hand, but he taped it to the girl and slathered it with wheat paste. I can't wait to see how he paints his people when the papier-mâché dries.

Ajax and PB and J were over at the sculpture table gathered around Mr. Joe, who was cutting an opening in a butter tub. "That's where the light will shine out," Mr. Joe explained to them.

"What light?" Ajax asked.

"The light from the flashlight I'm going to stick inside the oatmeal box," Mr. Joe answered.

"I know what it is," Matthew announced. "It's a lighthouse."

"That's right. I'm going to paint it with red and white stripes," Mr. Joe said. "And see this?" He taped together parts of one small round container and the corner of a square container to form a rowboat. "Then, I'm going to put the whole thing in this," he said, picking up the aluminum pan that still had a soggy layer of wheat paste. I'll paint the boat brown and the deepest part of the pan blue. I'll shape the wheat paste into a slope and sprinkle it with sand to make a beach. All I need is some chain and an anchor."

"I know!" Ajax shouted. "We could ask Mr. Gus the Lion Man to make an anchor."

I had heard about the Lion Man when I saw Ajax's lions on the Trellert's back porch. "Ajax, that's a great idea!" Mr. Joe said. "In fact, I'll ask Gus to make a little red-haired girl to put in the boat. How 'bout we clean up the yard, then pick up some pizzas? We can invite the Lion Man for pizza . . ."

"At his house!" Ajax interrupted.

"And I can ask him to help me finish up Kylie's night light," Mr. Joe finished.

I was invited, too, so I ran across the street to ask my parents if I could go to the Lion Man's. Of course, PB and J trailed after me shouting, "Can we go to the Lion Man's, too?" Miss Lisa, who had followed us, had to explain that one. Fortunately, I was allowed to go. Unfortunately, so were PB and J.

Back at the Trellert's, we flew around the yard packing up supplies, weighing down sculptures, and putting trash in big bags.

Over pizza, I asked Mr. Gus if he had gone to Goode Elementary, like me. "No," he explained, "I went to Smallwood School. That's where Black kids went. "We were called the Smallwooders," Mr. Gus continued.

"That's a funny name," said Ajax.

"You should talk about funny names," I teased. Then I asked Mr. Gus, "Where'd you live?"

"Newberry Street, and not everyone was glad to see us. I don't remember too much about it. Just heard my mama and pap talking in whispers at night. Then, one night—we young 'uns were supposed to be sleeping, but you now how it is." Mr. Gus winked at Ajax. "Me and my brother, we sneaked out of bed and looked out the window. The house was on a hill, and we lived on the third floor. We could see a long way, and we saw this glowing light in the sky."

"Was it a UFO?" I asked.

"I wish it was. It was the last night of a Klan convention."

"What's that?" Matthew asked.

"Well, now, that isn't a pretty story."

"But, it's an important one," Mr. Joe said. Turning to us, Mr. Joe explained, "The Klan was a group—actually, still is—that was against people who were Jewish or Black."

"Black, like us?" Pembrook couldn't believe this.

"Like Martin Luther King?" Janalia added. "Everybody loves him. He's a holiday!"

"And he had a dream," Ajax added.

"He dreamed about children of all races together—just like all you here on my porch," Mr. Gus began. "We heard later there were hundreds of people marching. They were all covered with sheets."

"Like ghosts?" asked Matthew.

"Worse," Mr. Gus explained.

"What about the light in the sky?" I asked.

"That was a cross. They set it on fire," Mr. Gus said.

"Set a cross on fire!" Ajax exploded. "They didn't like Jesus either?"

"I don't suppose they did," Mr. Gus sighed. "That's what I saw from my window. The sky was glowing 'cause a sixty-foot-high cross was set on fire, along with fifteen smaller crosses."

Everyone was quiet. "Thanks for the history lesson," Mr. Joe said.

"Yeah, those were plenty hard times," Mr. Gus went on. "Not long after that, my pap lost his job, like most folks. We scrapped and scraped and somehow got through."

"The Great Depression?" Stephen asked.

"Sure enough."

"Didn't you ever do anything fun?" Janalia asked.

"Sure," Mr. Gus answered. "We went to the fair."

"Like us!" PB and J piped up.

"One night," Mr. Gus brightened, "when I was a young feller, I had me a date so I got all gussied up. We went to the high school to hear Marian Anderson sing. They wouldn't let her sing at that fancy hall in D.C., but she sang here. And I married that girl."

"You married Marian Anderson?" I burst out.

"No," Mr Gus laughed. "I married the girl I took to the concert that night."

"Right there?" Matthew asked. "It would be cool to get married at a concert."

"No, no, I went off to the war first."

"With knights and javelins and spears?" Ajax asked.

Mr. Gus chuckled, "Hardly. World War II, complete with ships and planes and tanks. Now, enough about me. How 'bout we show Nikki and Pembrook and Janalia a few of my creations?"

While we enjoyed Mr. Gus' toys, Mr. Joe showed him the rowboat and sandy shore in a metal pan and explained his idea for Kylie's nightlight.

Mr. Gus grinned, "Come back next week, and I'll have it all ready."

A week later, I went to the Trellerts to see Matthew's sculptures. The boy had on a huge shirt that Matthew must have decorated. It was wild with fabric paint in bright reds, blues, and black. The girl was wrapped in a shimmering cloth—green and orange, like emerald rays of sunshine. Her palette was splashed with thick dabs of paint.

We were waiting for Mr. Joe to get home from work so we could go to the Lion Man's. This time, thankfully, PB and J had to stay home. When Mr. Joe came home, he handed a bag to Matthew. In it, there was black beret—the kind that artists wear. "I've been combing thrift shops during my lunch breaks looking for this," Mr. Joe said.

Matthew didn't say anything, but I could tell, by the careful way he arranged it on the boy's head, that he liked it.

After a flurry in the kitchen, we piled into the Trellert's van. We arrived at Mr. Gus's doorstep with an overflowing picnic basket. Before we started eating, Mr. Gus brought out the rowboat. It had a metal chain that was attached to a perfect little anchor that was rooted in the sandy shore. Inside the boat, there was a little girl with the curliest red hair and the widest grin.

"It's her! It's Kylie!" Ajax shouted.

"It sure is," Ethan added.

"She's beautiful," Miss Lisa said.

"Just like Kylie," Stephen added.

"And I made this." Mr. Gus held out a wooden plaque. We crowded around to look at it. The wood was smooth and shiny. There was a tiny lighthouse in every corner, and a ripple of waves made a border around the edges. In the middle were these words, which Miss Lisa read aloud:

"We have this as a sure and steadfast anchor of the soul, a hope that enters into the inner place behind the curtain, where Jesus has gone as a forerunner on our behalf . . ." (Hebrews 6:19–20).

"So she'll know," Mr. Gus explained, "that whatever storms come her way, Jesus has planted her anchor, and her boat will get safely to heaven's shore. Of course, she won't understand it all yet . . ." his voice trailed off.

"But what a verse for her to grow up with and grow into," Mr. Joe said.

"Gus," Miss Lisa looked up from the plaque she had been reading. "How can we ever thank you?"

"You can thank me by passing me the chicken salad," Mr. Gus mumbled.

"Why don't we get the girls and give this to Kylie now?" Ajax asked.

We all looked at Mr. Gus, who said, "Why not?"

"I'll go get them," Miss Lisa offered.

While Miss Lisa was gone, we set up Kylie's display. Mr. Gus rearranged his shelves to make room for the lighthouse-and-shore-in-a-metal-pan. He put them on a shelf that was low enough, but not too obvious. By the time Molly and Kylie arrived, we were all back on the front porch. Mr. Gus and Stephen were playing a game of chess. Ethan stretched out his arms, and Kylie flew into his lap, giggling. Ajax and Molly were jumping up and down, begging Mr. Gus to take them inside.

"Not yet." Mr. Gus pretended to be irritated. "Give me a few minutes to lose this chess game."

"C'mon, Mr. Gus," Ajax insisted. "You can lose any old day. I want to see your toys."

"You could resign," Stephen grinned.

"All right," Mr. Gus said. "I give up. Come on in!"

Molly ran to the Christmas scene she remembered from her first visit. She tapped the button, and the sparkling tree spun around. Kylie ran to the circus that had been her favorite. She punched the button and giggled as the clown tumbled off the diving board. Ajax and Matthew jumped up and down. The rest of us watched Kylie.

"Look!" Ajax burst out.

Kylie looked around. Spotting the lighthouse, she squealed with delight. She grinned big enough to light the sky. "It's the lighthouse." And she clapped her hands and shrieked, "Oh, it's me in the boat!"

Mr. Joe opened the door of the lighthouse and showed Kylie how to turn on the flashlight. Mr. Gus turned off the overhead light so the glow of the lighthouse shone.

"Oh, Oh, Oh!" Kylie exclaimed, crinkling her nose and reaching up toward the light. "I'll never be scared again."

"Well, you probably will be. That's why I made you this." Mr. Gus handed Kylie the plaque and read the verse to her.

"That means Jesus goes before his people. He has gone into heaven and dropped our anchor there." Mr. Gus tugged on the chain, but the anchor held fast where he had pinned it into the pan under the sandy beach.

"So, even when we have terrible storms here," Mr. Joe tossed the little row boat around on the painted sea, "we are anchored to a safe place. And, in all our storms, his light shines in the darkness."

Kylie jumped into Mr. Gus' arms. She grabbed his cheeks and smothered him with kisses. Mr. Gus laughed, "You better thank Mr. Joe, too. He made the lighthouse and the boat."

Kylie hopped down and ricocheted into Mr. Joe's arms. "I even can't wait to go to sleep in the dark tonight," she declared.

What a Mess!

Joe

I LEFT THE COURTHOUSE and walked slowly down the hot city street toward the spot where I had parked the car. Cutting through the alley, I heard the sound of children yelling. As the words became clearer, they caught my attention.

"Ugly mutts!" a boy's voice taunted.

"Curly furheads," another voice hissed.

When I heard a sound like the yelp of a dog, I changed my path and started running. I spun around the corner to see two boys stooped low. The boys heard my footsteps and took off, revealing Molly and Kylie huddled on the ground. Molly was holding her elbow and wailing.

Feeling torn, I yelled to Kylie, "Help your sister. I'll be right back." I took off after the boys and quickly caught up to them. I took each boy by the arm and hurried them back to the girls. Still holding the boys, I barked, "Give me your full names."

The boys were silent.

"Before I call the police," I warned.

"Cody," the bigger boy mumbled.

"Full name," I commanded.

"Cody Miller," he added.

"Brandon Thomas," said the other boy.

"Cody Miller and Brandon Thomas," I began, "one move from either of you, and I'll have the cops here in no time flat."

"Yeah!" Kylie yelled, glaring at the boys. I squatted down and set Molly on my knee. I pulled my silk handkerchief from my suit pocket, trying to decide whether to wipe Molly's runny nose or her bloody elbow. I handed her the handkerchief, and she wiped her nose. She curled against me, heaving with sobs.

"As for you two," I turned back to the boys, "do you know where I just came from?"

No answer. "I came from court. Maybe I should take you there right now and let the judge talk some sense into you."

Both boys shook their heads.

"Or we could go right down to the police station."

The boys' eyes grew wide.

"Let me get all the information I need, in case I have to make a police report." I shifted Molly so I could fumble through my jacket pocket. Notebooks often came in handy on interpreting assignments, and I knew I had a notebook and pen somewhere.

Finding them, I tried to take notes while holding Molly, who was still wailing. I turned to Kylie, "These the same boys who have been bothering you all year?"

Kylie nodded her head.

"We'll just have to make sure they learn their lesson this time," I said grimly. "Cody Miller, how old are you?"

"Nine," Cody answered.

"And you, Brandon Thomas?"

"Eight."

I asked the boys for their addresses and phone numbers, which I scribbled in my notebook. My knees were beginning to burn, and I wondered how much longer I could squat with Molly on my knee. Molly's cuts were bleeding onto my suit, and she was still bawling in my ear.

"Cody, who do you live with?" I continued my interrogation.

"My little sister, my little brother, my cousin."

"Who's in charge?" I growled.

"My grandma," Cody answered.

"And you, Brandon?"

"My mom."

"Now," I said, "I'm going to try these phone numbers you gave me. This is your last chance to tell me the truth. If these numbers don't work, I'll call the police."

"Sometimes mine works. Sometimes it don't. Depends on if my mom pays the bill," Brandon said.

"Okay, if yours doesn't work, we'll go to your house before I call the police." I handed my notebook and pen to Kylie and shifted Molly again, so I could find my phone. "Your grandma and your mom, they both speak English?" I asked the boys.

Cody and Brandon nodded. I began to punch in the numbers. "What's your grandma's last name?" I asked Cody.

"Same as mine," Cody said, looking at the ground.

"Hello, is this Ms. Miller? Is this the home of Cody Miller?" Cody listened nervously as I talked to his grandmother.

"No, this is not the police, ma'am. But Cody has gotten himself into trouble bullying some little girls."

Cody's toe wiggled through a hole in his shoe while I listened to his grandmother's woes. "I understand how it is, ma'am."

I half-listened while I shifted my weight again. Molly's wails had subsided to snuffling, and I was beginning to think more clearly. I thought back to the court case I had just left. The defendant had been ordered to do community service. "Ma'am, what if I arranged a little community service for Cody?"

When she agreed, I closed the conversation, "Then I'll call you soon to make the arrangements."

One more call. My good black suit was a mess of sweat, blood, and dirt. I stood Molly on the street and struggled to my feet. Ms. Thomas was at work, according to the teenager who answered the phone. The television in the background was so loud I had to ask three times before I understood that she would be home around six o'clock. "Thank you. I'll call her then," I shouted.

"You boys can go now. I'll be visiting your homes soon," I said. The boys took off running.

"Thanks, Joey!" Kylie hopped into my arms.

"You two are next," I said sternly.

"Us? We didn't do nothin' wrong," Kylie said.

"Oh, yes, you did. What are you doing out by yourselves this far from home? Does your grandma know where you are?"

"We wanted to go to a store 'cause we have all this," Kylie opened her fist to display a handful of coins. "It's Mama's birthday, and this is what we didn't spend on the lions 'cause Mr. Gus gave us them for free."

"If you want to go to the store, ask someone. If it's a surprise for your mama, ask your grandma," I scolded.

"But Grandma would have said no," Kylie said.

"Then you'd just have to make something," I went on.

"But," Kylie protested, "we don't got no paper or markers or nothin'."

"You could have asked Lisa. Anything but wandering around by yourselves. No arguing. No going out without permission. Ever. If you ever do this again . . ." I began.

"You'll call the cops?" Kylie asked, eyes wide.

"Worse. I'll call Child Protective Services, and that will mean terrible trouble. I'll talk to your mom and grandma about that, then I'm sure they'll read you the riot act."

"What's that mean?" Kylie asked.

"You'll find out tonight, when your mom gets home from work," I sighed.

Molly started crying again. "They said I was ugly."

"Molly," I began. "Tell you what, we'll stop at your house to ask your grandma if you can come to my house . . ."

"Yippee!" Kylie shouted.

"Only for a minute," I warned. "You can't stay and play because you didn't ask permission to leave your house. In fact, you won't come over all week. Or all weekend. That's your punishment for going out without asking. My part, at least. There'll be more from your mom. I'm sure of that. This can't ever happen again."

Now Kylie was wailing. Back at the girls' house, I stood on the stoop talking to their grandma. Kylie was still having her tantrum in the car. I warned that if she did not stop screaming, I would not take her to our house at all. She screamed louder. I picked her up and carried her into her house, while she pounded her fists on my chest.

When I pulled up to our house, I set Molly on the stoop. "Lisa?" I shouted, as I stormed through the front door.

Lisa took one look at my suit, which was soaked, filthy, and rumpled and exclaimed, "What a mess!"

"Pretty much sums up my day," I answered. "And Molly's was even worse." I pointed to the front steps, where Molly had started sobbing again. Lisa ran to Molly, but I marched through the living room, dining room, and kitchen. I grabbed a pair of scissors and went out to the backyard where Matthew was building a castle in the sandbox.

As I began cutting flowers from the strip of garden that

lines the side of our yard, Matthew asked—rather peevishly—what I was doing. I couldn't deal with Matthew now but just kept snipping flowers. When I went back through the house, Matthew followed me. I sat down with Molly on the front steps and picked up one of the flowers I had clutched in my hand—a pink petunia with crimson streaks. "Molly," I said, giving her the flower. "What color is this flower?"

"Pink," Molly answered.

"Pink is your favorite color, isn't it?" I asked.

Molly nodded. "It's pretty," Molly whispered.

I handed Molly another flower. It looked like the pink one, but it was a velvety red.

"This one's red," Molly said. "And pretty."

"How can this one be pretty?" I argued. "It's not pink."

"But it's still pretty," Molly said.

One by one, I handed Molly all the flowers. Painted daisies and purple pansies. Peach hollyhocks and lemon day lilies. Molly named their colors and said how pretty they were. I argued, "How can that one be pretty," I pointed to a peony in Molly's lap, "when it doesn't look anything like this one?" I handed her the purple lavender. "One is short and round and white as the clouds. The other is tall and thin and purple. And neither of them is pink."

Molly giggled. "They just are. They're all pretty."

"It's the same with people," I said, pointing to Matthew, who was watching from the front doorway. "He has beautiful tan skin, shining brown eyes, and straight black hair. He doesn't look anything like Ajax, who has beautiful brown skin, eyes that laugh, and curly black hair. Ethan has straight blond hair and blue eyes, and Stephen has wavy brown hair and gray eyes. Some of them must be ugly, right? 'Cause they look so different from each other, and people who look different are ugly, right?"

"No!" Molly laughed.

I went on, "God made all the flowers different for his glory. And he made all the people different for his glory, too." I held up a marigold. "This one is the color of fire, like Kylie's hair. It can't be pretty, can it? We should just throw it away."

"No!" Molly shouted, grabbing the flower. "It is pretty."

We went on comparing colors and sizes and petals. Molly

giggled as she sifted through the flowers on her lap. Finally I gave her the last flower. A short stem held one creamy pink rose and a tiny rosebud.

I asked, "Do you know what kind of flower this is, Molly?" Molly shook her head.

"A rose," Matthew said.

"That's right, Matthew," I went on. "All the flowers are pretty, but I like this rose best of all. Do you know why, Molly?" Molly looked at me and waited.

"It reminds me of you. You're a beautiful little rose. Our Molly Rose. You're like this little flower here." I pointed to the bud. "And God is helping you grow into this beautiful rose."

The door slammed as Matthew ran into the house. He came back with a vase full of water—sloshing a stream of spilt water behind him. He held out the vase and asked, "Can she keep it, Dad? To take her flowers home?"

"Way to be a man!" I grinned at him as he gave the vase to Molly.

CHAPTER 19

Born for the Roller Coaster

Matthew

AT DINNER THAT NIGHT, we talked about Cody and Brandon. "Make them clean up after Fluffernutter in the backyard," Ethan suggested. "That'd teach them."

"No fair! That's your job!" I yelled.

"Maybe they could do all of our chores. All summer!" Stephen said.

"Make them build us a new house. A mansion." I always have good ideas.

"A castle!" Ajax shouted.

"That's it!" Mom exclaimed. Everyone stared at her.

"Really?" I asked.

"Not quite," Mom said. "But, to teach them to treat the girls like princesses, have them build a castle for Molly and Kylie in their backyard. All the girls have is that strip of concrete out back, with nothing to do. We've got some outdoor carpeting we could put inside. And we could do a Bible study with them about God being our refuge. We could get books out of the library about castles."

"We could paint it silver!" I shouted.

"And shoot attackers with bows and arrows!" Ajax added.

"No bows and arrows, but let's see what we can come up with," Dad said, pushing away from the dinner table. So, Ajax and I had to clear the dishes, while Stephen and Ethan helped Dad draw the plans.

The next morning, I had another good idea, so I brought my money box downstairs. "Absolutely not," Mom yelled. "No money box at the breakfast table."

"But, Mom," I cried. "I want to . . ."

"No arguing. Put it away."

I stomped up the stairs carrying my money box. Halfway up the stairs, I dropped it. There was a loud bang, then my coins crashed down the stairs. Ajax ran out of the living room and slid on the coins that were all over the floor of the front hall. He slid into Fluffernutter, who began barking.

"Nobody touch my money!" I yelled. Fluffer barked louder. Ethan came down the stairs to see what was wrong. He tripped over Ajax's foot, and tumbled to the floor.

"Don't touch my money!" I said again.

"What's going on?" Stephen complained from the top of the stairs. "You woke me up. Maybe," he said to himself, "if I go back to sleep, this will turn out to be just a bad dream."

"No, just a typical morning at the Trellerts," Dad said.

And, just like that, they were all laughing. I stuffed my coins into my money box and shouted, "You're laughing at me!"

I ran upstairs. I heard Dad say, "Okay, boys, go eat breakfast."

Dad and Mom came up to my room. "I was trying to do something good," I said, "and you're ruining everything."

"What were you trying to do, Matthew?" Mom asked.

"It's a surprise," I said.

"I thought you hated surprises," Dad began.

"Not when I'm in charge of them," I yelled.

"So, what's the surprise? You were planning on giving your money to the poor?" Dad asked.

I told him, "We are the poor."

"No more complaining," Dad said. "Now what about the surprise?"

"I'll show you when it's done. You'll like it. I promise. Please take me to the store to get the stuff I need. That's why I brought my money box down."

"You're going to spend your own money?" Mom asked. I nodded.

"The money you've been saving all year?" Dad asked.

I nodded again.

"What kind of things do you want to buy?"

"Things for the surprise," I explained.

Mom and Dad did not look very sure about this. So I said, "Not a feather boa. Not a wig with long blonde hair. Not ballet slippers covered with sparkles. Not any of the things that you won't let me buy."

"Let Mom and me talk and pray a few minutes," Dad said. "Go eat breakfast, so we can get Cody and Brandon. I'll be stopping at the store anyhow to get some things for the castle."

An hour later, we trooped after Dad who was coming up from the basement with boards, tools, and the plans for the castle. We piled in the van, with boards sticking out every which way. Dad drove us to the store, where I ran off to buy things for my surprise, while Dad, Stephen, Ethan, and Ajax went off to get everything on their castle-making list. I had already paid for my stuff when they got to the register. I had gotten three bags and put the stuff I bought in one bag, which I put inside the other one, and inside the last bag, so no one could see through them. I held my bags tightly closed. When we got to the car, I hid my bags under the seat.

Cody and Brandon were both on Cody's porch. As they climbed in the van, Cody's grandma said, "Mind you listen now, boys."

"Oh, they'll listen, ma'am," Dad said.

We spent the morning building the walls and laying the floor of the castle. It was fun, even though Dad kept preaching about the castle and the way he wanted Cody and Brandon to treat the girls. "They are children of the King, and you better treat them like royalty."

"Yes, sir," Cody said.

When Mom came by with lunch, Cody and Brandon proudly pointed to nails they had hammered. As if that was anything special. Molly and Kylie bopped from Stephen's lap to Ethan's lap. I even let them sit on my lap—for a minute. When Brandon asked for a drink, Kylie jumped on top of the cooler, so Brandon couldn't get a drink.

"Kylie, come with me," Mom said.

By the time Kylie came back, all the boys were back at work. "You're doin' good, Brandon," Kylie said. "You too, Cody," she added.

By four o'clock, the castle was finished except for all the good stuff like paint and glitter. Kylie asked to come to our house but Dad told her she still wasn't allowed. She pouted, but Dad said if she didn't thank Brandon and Cody, it would be a long time before she ever came back to our house. So she shouted her thanks and even blew kisses when we drove away. At Cody's house, Dad talked with Cody's grandma. He told her he'd be back next Saturday so the boys could finish their "community service."

"Great job, Cody!" Dad said. "You did a man's job today. And you did it well!"

At Brandon's house, Dad went on about Brandon, too. "Gonna have yourself a fine young man before long," Dad told Brandon's mom, giving Brandon a high five and a thumbs up.

When Dad got back to the van, Ajax said, "Next week, we'll build a drawbridge and a moat." Ajax is big on castles.

"Whoa!" Dad shouted. "Turrets and silver paint, yes. Drawbridge and moat, absolutely not."

Later that night, I asked Dad to show me how to use the washer and dryer. After he showed me, he just stood there. Like I was supposed to unpack my surprise in front of him. "Now, would you leave?" I asked. He frowned. "Please?" I added.

An hour later, Mom came down to the basement. I popped up from the stool I had pulled in front of the dryer. "What are you doing down here?" I said, only it came out a yell. The only thing in the basement is the laundry and Dad's tools, and Dad's office. Dad calls the basement his man cave. Mom calls it the dungeon. Dad always does the laundry, and Mom never comes down here. Well, almost never.

"I just came to check on you. And to tell you it's almost bedtime," Mom said.

"I'm almost done," I said. "Then I'll come up."

"Deal," Mom agreed and went back upstairs.

When the dryer went off, I took my bag and held it in front of the dryer door. I looked around to make sure no one was watching. I opened the dryer and stuffed the surprise into the bag. Then into the second bag. Then into the third bag. I folded the top of the bag down again and again. Then I ran all the way to the third floor and hid the bags in my closet. I ran back down to the kitchen.

"Matthew," Mom shouted. "Time for bed."

"I'm coming," I called, "but don't go in my room yet. Please."

I poked through the kitchen cupboards until I found what I wanted. I grabbed a few more bags and put the stuff inside. I ran to my room and put the bag in the closet.

After church the next day, I stayed in my room all afternoon. I went downstairs for dinner, but I ate fast, then ran back to my room. I tried to sneak to the kitchen to get something, but Mom caught me. She asked what I wanted, but I just shook my head. After she left, I stuffed something up my shirt and ran back to the third floor.

The next afternoon, I finished. "When will we see Molly and Kylie again?" I asked Mom.

"Saturday," Mom answered. "Dad will be taking all you kids and Cody and Brandon there to finish the castle."

"Won't you be coming?" I asked.

"I'll come by with lunch, just like last week," Mom answered.

"Okay," I said. "I'll show my surprise then."

Saturday morning, I was the first one up and dressed. I had my surprise wrapped and hidden in a paper bag. When we got to the girls' house, I tucked the bag under a seat in the van, then put a blanket on top of it. We built the turrets, painted the castle, and nailed the rug on the floor. Molly and Kylie helped paint the castle.

"Mom's here!" I shouted. She set the picnic basket on the back porch and began to say how nice the castle looked. "Hurry!" I yelled to Dad. "Open the van!"

I got my bag and carried it to the back porch. Now that it was finally time, I felt scared. What if Mom and Dad didn't like my surprise? What if Molly didn't like my surprise? I shoved the bag at Molly and held my breath.

Molly opened the bag and pulled out the gift I had wrapped. I wrapped it in paper I had colored myself. White paper covered with flowers, like all the flowers Dad showed her that day she was crying on our porch. Molly opened the paper and pulled out a pink sundress. Her mouth opened wide, like she was very happy. Mom gasped when she saw the tiny rosebuds all over the dress. Each pocket of the dress had a rose in bloom.

Molly said, "It's the prettiest dress I ever saw!"

Mom said, "Those flowers are the loveliest shade of

crimson, and the emerald green stems and leaves are perfect!"

Kylie clapped her hands, "It's pretty, Molly. Just like you. And when you get big, it will be my turn to wear it."

Molly threw her arms around me. I let her hug me. She just kept on hugging. Finally, I patted her back a few times.

Dad said, "Matthew, it's the prettiest dress I've ever seen. Did you make those flowers?"

I nodded. "How?" Stephen asked.

"I bought the dress and used fabric paints and Mom's cake decorating kit. I put the fabric paint in the icing bag and squeezed out the flowers. I kept looking at the pictures in the cake book. I practiced on old rags, then I made the dress. And look," I pulled something else out of the bag.

It was a pink cap that I had decorated with rosebuds.

Missy came out to see what all the noise was about. She couldn't believe I decorated the dress myself. "Mama, can I wear it now?" Molly asked.

"After you finish your lunch," Missy said.

"Lunch!" Mom gasped. She had forgotten all about it, but Dad was already passing out the sandwiches and drinks.

Molly hardly ate anything. "I am finished," she yelled, running into the house to change her clothes. A few minutes later, Molly came out twirling around in her new dress. Her brown hair curled out from under her cap. She threw her arms around me—again—and shouted, "Thanks!"

After lunch, we packed up the tools, the scraps of wood, and the empty paint cans. Mom packed up lunch. We took Cody and Brandon to their homes and made plans to take them to the city pool next week.

Back home, Ajax dragged his lions out to the backyard to guard his soccer goal and boasted, "I'm goin' to whip you at soccer today, Ethan!" Stephen was reading. I sat in the living room while Mom and Dad hurried around, doing whatever moms and dads hurry around doing.

Finally, Mom noticed me sitting alone in the living room. "What's up?" she asked.

"I didn't get anything," I said.

"What do you mean?" she asked.

"Ajax got the lions. Kylie got the lighthouse. Molly got the dress. But I didn't get anything. And now I don't have any money either."

We sat there quietly a minute. "Matthew," Mom began. "How did you feel when you saw Molly crying after Cody and Brandon were so mean to her?"

"She was crying bad. I felt awful," I said.

Mom went on, "And, how did you feel when you saw Molly dancing around looking so beautiful in the dress you made for her?"

"Good," I said.

"Molly shines in the dress you made for her. God gave you a gift, Matthew. He made you good at art. You saw what Molly needed and helped her in a way that no one else could. You were a real man for her today."

"Me? A real man?" I asked. "Not just Cody and Brandon with all their hammering, and Stephen and Ethan with all their sawing?"

"Yes, you. Especially you."

I felt happy for a minute, then sad again. "It's hard being a man," I said.

"Real hard," Mom nodded. "How do you think Dad felt when he took you over to Mr. Gus's that first time? Or when he chased after Cody and Brandon and called their homes?"

"Yeah, there's a lot of scary to being a man," I said sadly.

"But," Mom went on, "how did each of you men feel today?"

Dad walked into the room. "Today was an ups day for being a man, right, Matthew? It's like that card game you made up when you were little." I looked at him, confused. "Remember? You asked me to play a card game you made up. You said it was called Ups or Downs and asked me which I wanted to be. I made the mistake of picking downs. You played with all the cards a long time, moving them from one pile to another. I didn't get to do anything. Finally, you told me you had won. When I said I hadn't even got a turn yet, you said, 'Ups is better.' Well, there are a lot of ups and downs to living as a man. But today was an ups day."

"Speaking of ups and downs," Mom said. "Do you remember how scared you were the first time you rode a roller coaster?"

"I screamed the whole time," I laughed.

"I had nail marks on my arms for a week because of the way you clung to me," Dad added.

Mom went on, "Did you decide you like roller coasters?"

"I was born for roller coasters!" I grinned.

"Well," Dad hugged me. "Sometimes, being a man is like riding a roller coaster. And you were born for that roller coaster, too."

Chapter Discussions

Chapter 1: Lions for Ajax

1. Why do some boys make fun of Kylie and Molly?

2. What is Lisa's response to the boys who are mistreating Molly and Kylie?
   (See Matthew 5:43–45; Romans 12:14, 17–21.)

3. What did Christ do for people who were his enemies?
   (See Romans 5:8.)

4. What does it mean to show respect or honor? (See Matthew 7:12; Romans 12:10; Philippians 2:3; 1 Peter 2:17.)

5. In what ways do characters in this chapter either respect and honor others or fail to do so?

Chapter 2: Polite in Three Languages

1. Why are good manners important?
   (See 1 Corinthians 13:4–5.)

2. Why should we respect and honor God? (See Psalm 47:7–9; Isaiah 6:3; Romans 11:33–36; Revelation 4:11.)

3. Why should we respect and honor other people?
   (See Genesis 1:26–27; James 3:9–10.)

4. How did Jesus respect and honor God? (See John 12:49, 14:31; Philippians 2:8).

5. How can we have power to respect and honor others when we don't feel like doing so? (See Galatians 2:20; Ephesians 4:22–24.)

Chapter 3: Bullies Foiled

1. How do Stephen and Ethan respond to the boys who are mistreating Molly and Kylie? (See Isaiah 1:17; Zechariah 7:9–10; Philippians 2:4.)

2. Why is it important to show respect to people of cultural backgrounds that are different from our own? (See Genesis 1:27; Acts 17:26; Romans 15:7.)

3. In what ways did characters in this chapter treat others with respect?

4. In what ways did characters in this chapter treat others with disrespect?

Chapter 4: Reeling in Matthew

1. Why did Matthew feel "icky"?

2. Why do people feel shame? (See Genesis 3:8–10; Daniel 9:3–10.)

3. What did Christ do on the cross? (See Colossians 1:21–22; Hebrews 12:1–2.)

4. What happens to the shame of every person who believes in Christ and turns from sin? (See Isaiah 61:7; Colossians 2:11–15.)

Chapter 5: Gotcha Day

1. How did Matthew and Ajax join the Trellert family?

2. How does God bring people into his family? (See Romans 8:14–17; Ephesians 1:3–14.)

3. How did Kylie misuse the gift she was given?

4. How should we use all the gifts God gives us? (See 1 Corinthians 10:31; 1 Timothy 4:4, 6:17–19.)

Chapter 6: Thanks for the Tickets

1. What is God's plan for marriage?
   (See Genesis 2:18–25; Matthew 19:4–6; Ephesians 5:22–33.)
2. What is God's plan for children and parents?
   (Deuteronomy 6:6–7; Psalm 78:2–8; Ephesians 6:1–4;
   Hebrews 12:5–13.)
3. Why is gratitude to God important? (See Romans 1:21;
   Ephesians 5:19–20; Colossians 3:15–17; 1 Thessalonians 5:16–18.)
4. Why is it important to show grateful appreciation for other
   people? (See Matthew 7:12; Romans 12:10, 16:1–16.)

Chapter 7: Cockroach or Superhero

1. What is Lisa's response to the boys who are mistreating Molly
   and Kylie? (See Ephesians 4:13–15; 2 Timothy 2:24–26.)
2. How should we respond when we do something wrong?
   (See 1 John 1:8–10.)
3. Why is it important for children to learn to obey? (See
   Proverbs 19:16; Luke 11:28; John 14:15–17; Ephesians 6:1–3.)
4. What is Matthew's attitude toward money?
5. What does God say should be our attitude toward money?
   (See Luke 12:13–31; 1 Timothy 6:6–10; Hebrews 13:5–6.)

Chapter 8: Backward and Forward

1. How has God shone his light in the world?
   (See 2 Corinthians 4:6.)
2. What happens when God shines his light into our hearts?
   (See John 8:12; Ephesians 1:16–21; 1 John 1:6–7.)
3. What does it mean to build your house on the rock of
   Jesus Christ? (See Deuteronomy 11:18–28; Luke 6:46–49;
   Hebrews 12:28.)
4. How did Stephen and Ethan fail to love and respect
   Matthew?

Chapter 9: A Thirteen Pencil Day

1. How can we be assured that God exists?
   (See Psalm 19:1–11; John 14:9; Romans 1:20.)
2. What can we do with our doubts and questions about God?
   (See Psalm 77; Mark 9:23–24.)
3. What does God say about giving? (See Luke 6:38, 12:32–34.)
4. How does Matthew fail to trust God?
5. Why can we trust God to care for us?
   (See Matthew 6:25–34; Romans 8:28–30.)

Chapter 10: Best Bits

1. In this chapter, what gives Ajax joy? (See Acts 20:35;
   1 Timothy 6:17–19; Hebrews 13:16.)
2. Why is it sometimes hard to love people?
   (See Romans 3:23; Galatians 5:19–21; James 4:1–4.)
3. What does God say about loving others?
   (See 1 Corinthians 13; 1 John 4:7–21.)
4. Where can we find power when it is hard to love others?
   (See Romans 6:3–14; Philippians 2:12–13; 2 Timothy 1:7.)

Chapter 11: Milk and Miracles

1. What is missions? (See Genesis 22:17–18; 1 Chronicles
   16:23–24; Matthew 28:18–20; John 10:16; Romans 15:20–21.)
2. Who decides where we will be born and where we will
   live? (See Psalm 139:16; Acts 17:24–27.)
3. How are people different from animals?
   (See Genesis 1:24–31; Psalm 8:4–9.)
4. Why did God create people as male and female?
   (See Genesis 2:15–23; Isaiah 43:7.)
5. Why is it important that Jesus is both God and human? (See
   Romans 8:3–4; Colossians 1:19–23; Hebrews 2:14–18, 7:23–28.)
6. What does it mean to be joined with Christ by
   faith and how does that impact your daily life?
   (See John 15:5; Romans 6; Galatians 2:20.)

Chapter 12: A Crack in the Concrete

1. What is Matthew struggling to understand?
2. Why are there so many difficult and painful things in this world? (See Genesis 3; Romans 5:12–14, 8:20–22.)
3. What are some good things God does through the hard things of life? (See Romans 5:3–5, 8:28–30; 2 Corinthians 4:16–18; James 1:2–4; 1 Peter 1:3–7.)
4. What does your family mean to you? (See Psalms 127–128.)

Chapter 13: Plunge Right In

1. What did Ajax do that was wrong?
2. What did Ajax do that was worthy of praise?
3. Why is it important to ask forgiveness when we sin against people? (See Matthew 5:23–24.)
4. What does it mean to forgive someone? (See Psalm 103:10–12; Matthew 18:21–35.)
5. Why should we forgive others? (See Matthew 6:9–15; Colossians 3:12–16.)

Chapter 14: Molly Speaks

1. What did Molly, Kylie, and Matthew do that was wrong?
2. When Joe and Lisa talked to the children about their disobedience, what did the children do?
3. What should we do when confronted about our sin? (See Acts 2:36–38; 1 John 1:8–9.)
4. What does God say about taking other people's possessions? (See Exodus 20:15; 1 Corinthians 6:9–11; Ephesians 4:28.)
5. Why do children sometimes need loving discipline? (See Proverbs 19:18, 22:6, 29:17; Hebrews 12:7–13.)

Chapter 15: Even Matthew Had the Sense

1. Why did Joe return to the Lion Man's home?
   (See Ephesians 5:25–30; 1 Corinthians 16:13–14.)

2. Why do you think Lisa wants to include the Lion Man in their family celebration? (See Romans 12:13b; Hebrews 13:1–3.)

3. What responsibilities does God give to fathers?
   (See Ephesians 6:1–4.)

4. What hope does the Bible offer to children who don't grow up with their fathers?
   (See Deuteronomy 10:17–18; Psalm 27:10, 68:5.)

Chapter 16: The Lighthouse

1. What does the Bible say about unexpected changes to our plans? (See Proverbs 16:1–3, 9; James 4:13–16.)

2. What does the Bible say about how "other" God is?
   (See Psalm 115:3; Isaiah 55:8–9.)

3. What does the Bible promise about how near God is during scary times? (See Psalm 23, 46:1–3; Isaiah 41:10, 43:1–2.)

4. What can "bestest days" remind us of? (See Romans 8:18; 1 Corinthians 2:9; Revelation 21:1–4, 22:1–5.)

Chapter 17: Light in the Dark

1. How do artists reflect God's image?
   (See Exodus 28:40, 31:2–5; Psalm 8:3; Colossians 1:16.)

2. How do people, created as male and female, reflect God's glory? (See Genesis 1–2.)

3. Why is hatred for groups of people so sinful?
   (See Isaiah 43:7; Revelation 5:9.)

4. What does it mean that Christ is an anchor for our souls?
   (See John 10:9, 11, 27–29; Philippians 3:12.)

Chapter 18: What a Mess!

1. How does Joe respond to the bullies?
    (See Micah 6:8; 1 Corinthians 16:13–14.)

2. How does Joe respond to Molly and Kylie?
    (See Proverbs 10:17, 15:32; Galatians 6:1–2.)

3. Why did God create people with such diversity?
    (See Isaiah 43:7; Revelation 5:9.)

4. How should we respond to the way God has created
    us physically? (See Psalm 139:13–16; Romans 8:17–25;
    1 Corinthians 15:50–53; Philippians 4:4–8.)

Chapter 19: Born for the Roller Coaster

1. How has Matthew grown and changed throughout this
    story?

2. How did the Trellerts help Cody and Brandon?

3. What did Cody and Brandon learn about being men?

4. What did Matthew learn about being a man?

Downloadable Study Guide

For a more in-depth consideration of these themes, please download and use the free 42-page study guide from the Publishers at the following link:

www.shepherdpress.com/products/lions-for-ajax

THE GOSPEL FOR MOVING TARGETS: HELPING ACTIVE CHILDREN GROW IN GRACE

Nancy Snyder
Large-format (8.5 x 11)
Illustrated Otabind (lay-flat) book, 288pp | $24.99
ISBN: 978-1-63342-109-7

These hands-on devotional lessons are designed for children who struggle to sit still, keep quiet, pay attention, follow directions, and control their emotions.

These lessons are also designed to help parents and teachers who love such children aim the gospel at the hearts of moving targets.

Includes links to downloadable resource images from Shepherd Press website.

"...this is a book for all families. It is full of mature biblical wisdom and a real understanding of how Christian character is formed. Anyone who buys this book to help them love their children will find its teaching transforming them first of all. And that, of course, is exactly how God means family life to be."

—Sinclair Ferguson

"This book should prove useful to parents, grandparents, and anyone else working with small children."

—Jerry Bridges

About Shepherd Press Publications

- They are gospel driven.
- They are heart focused.
- They are life changing.

Our Invitation to You

We passionately believe that what we are publishing can be of benefit to you, your family, your friends, and your work colleagues. So we are inviting you to join our online mailing list so that we may reach out to you with news about our latest and forthcoming publications, and with special offers.

Visit:

www.shepherdpress.com/newsletter

and provide your name and email address.